ISSUES IN SOCIOLOGY
Edited by Robert G. Burgess

Women in Contemporary Society

Carol Buswell
*Senior Lecturer in Sociology,
Newcastle upon Tyne Polytechnic*

MACMILLAN

First published 1989

Published by
MACMILLAN EDUCATION LTD
Houndmills, Basingstoke, Hampshire RG21 2XS
and London
Companies and representatives
throughout the world

Original series design by Milford Hurley Graphic Design

Printed in Hong Kong

British Library Cataloguing in Publication Data
Buswell, Carol
Women in contemporary society. —— (Issues in
sociology).
1. Society. Role of women – Conference
proceedings
I. Title   II. Series
305.4′2
ISBN 0–333–46131–2

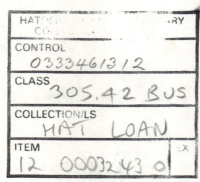

Contents

Series Editor's Preface		vi
Acknowledgements		vii
Introduction		1
1	Theories of sex and gender	5
2	The family – wives and mothers	21
3	Girls growing up	39
4	Education	53
5	Women and employment	71
6	Women and the media	91
7	Formal politics and trades unions	107
8	Women together	126
Bibliography		142
Index		146

Series Editor's Preface

The aim of the *Issues in Sociology* series is to provide easy access to debates and controversies in different fields of study within sociology. In particular, the series is designed for students who are beginning sociology as part of sixth form study or in further education, or in adult and continuing education classes.

The books in the series are written by authors who have wide experience of research and teaching in a special field of study where they have been directly involved in key debates. In this way, they are able to communicate the richness of the subject to the student. At the beginning of each volume, an introductory essay presents an outline of the field where key issues, problems and debates are identified. In subsequent chapters, the student is provided with commentaries, sets of materials, questions for discussion, essays and guides to further reading. The result is a workbook that can be used by the individual student or by teachers working with small groups or a whole class.

Altogether the material in each volume seeks to convey the way in which sociological research involves a knowledge of theory and method as well as detailed understanding of an area of study.

Many sociologists have recently been concerned with questions about women. The result is to extend our understanding of different areas of social life and to highlight the centrality of gender in sociological analysis. Carol Buswell has brought together a variety of source materials that will help students to extend and develop their understanding of women's experiences in a range of contexts. Her commentaries and questions will greatly help students to appreciate that women's concerns are as central to sociological studies as those of men.

Robert G. Burgess
University of Warwick

Acknowledgements

I am grateful to Bob Burgess and Mary Maynard whose comments on a draft of this book were most appreciated, especially as they were offered in such a friendly and constructive fashion. Special thanks to Terry Donnelly who cheerfully and extremely efficiently typed the drafts to fit my deadlines even though this was an extra job for her.

The authors and publishers wish to thank the following who have kindly given permission for the use of copyright material:

The Associated Examining Board, University of Cambridge Local Examinations Syndicate, University of Oxford Delegacy of Local Examinations and Welsh Joint Education Committee for questions from past examination papers.

Basil Blackwell Ltd for material from *Faces of Feminism* by Olive Banks, Martin Robertson, 1981, pp. 227, 228 and 229; *Divisions of Labour* by R. E. Pahl, pp. 78 and 79; and *Sweet Freedom* by Anna Coote and Beatrix Campbell, 1982, pp. 143, 149, 152, 153 and 167.

Richard Brown for material from 'Women as employees: some comments on research in industrial sociology' in D. Barker and S. Allen (eds), *Dependence and Exploitation in Work and Marriage* Longman, 1976, pp. 23, 24 and 25.

Comedia Publishing for material from *Family Television: Cultural Power and Domestic Leisure* by David Morley, 1986, pp. 147, 148, 149, 152, 153, 155, 157 and 158.

Betty Cook for material from *We Struggled to Laugh*, Barnsley Miners' Wives Action Group, 1987, pp. 10, 11, and 12.

Croom Helm for 'Working at the Superstore' by J. Kuhn in T. Scarlet *et al.* (eds), *Women, Work and Family: In Britain and Germany*, 1986, pp. 167 and 168.

Sue Finch for extract from 'Socialists – Feminists and Greenham', *Feminists Review, No. 23*, June 1986, pp. 96, 98–9.

Gower Publishing Company Ltd. for material from *Forever Feminine: Women's Magazines and the Cult of Femininity* by Marjorie Ferguson, Heinmann, 1983, pp. 184 and 185.

International Labour Office for material from *Microelectronics and Office Jobs: The Impact of the Chip on Women's Employment*, pp. 400–2. Copyright 1983 International Labour Organisation, Geneva.

The Controller of Her Majesty's Stationery Office for tables from *Social Trends 17*, 1987, and *Social Trends 18*, 1988, CSO; and *Women's Work Histories: An Analysis of the Women and Employment Survey*, DOE, Crown copyright.

Labour Research Department and Phil Evans for a cartoon from *Part-time Workers* by Phil Evans.

Macmillan Publishers Ltd for material from *Women in Politics* by Vicky Randall, 1982, pp. 66, 67 and 68.

Manchester University Press for material from 'Renegotiation of the Domestic Division of Labour in the Context of Male Redundancy' by Lydia Morris in B. Roberts *et al.* (eds), *New Approaches to Economic Life*, 1985, pp. 406 and 407.

National Westminster Bank PLC for material from 'The Changing Labour Market: The Phenomenon of Part-time Employment in Britain' by O. Robinson, *National Westminster Bank Quarterly Review*, Nov. 1985, pp. 20, 21, 22, 23 and 25.

Open University Press for material from 'Labour Market Structure and Work-force Divisions' by E. Garnsey, J. Ruberty and F. Wilkinson in R. Deem and G. Salman (eds), *Work, Culture and Society*, 1985, pp. 52, 53 and 54.

Penguin Books Ltd for material from *Double Identity: The lives of Working Mothers* by Sue Sharp, Penguin Books, 1984. Copyright © 1984 Sue Sharp, pp. 55 and 69.

Plenum Publishing Corporation for material from 'Three Female Roles in Television Commercials' by P. D. Mamay and R. L. Simpson, *Sex Roles*, 7, No. 12, 1981, pp. 1224 and 1225.

Routledge and Kegan Paul for material from *Social Researching* from C. Bell and H. Roberts, 1984, pp. 71, 72, 73, 74, 80 and 81; 'Biological Explanations in Sex-role Stereotypes' by J. Archer in J. Chetwynd and O. Harnet (eds), *The Sex Role System*, 1978, pp. 7

and 8; 'Resistances and Responses: The Experiences of Black Girls in Britain' in V. Amos and P. Parmar (eds), *Feminism for Girls*, 1981, pp. 140 and 141; and 'Sex Differences in Performance in Science Examinations' by J. Harding in R. Deem (ed.), *Schooling for Women's Work*, 1980, pp. 94 and 95.

Simon and Schuster Ltd for material from *Politics and Sexual Equality* by Pippa Norris, Wheatsheaf Books, 1987, pp. 115, 120, 121, 122, 123 and 124.

Social and Community Planning Research for table from British Social Attitudes Survey, 1987, cited in *British Social Attitudes: the 5th Report*, edited by Roger Jowell, Sharon Witherspoon and Lindsay Brook.

Tavistock Publications for material from *On Being a Woman* by F. Fransella and K. Frost, 1977, pp. 13, 14 and 15.

Trade Union Congress for material from *Images of Inequality: The Portrayal of Women in the Media*, p. 10.

Virago Press for material from *Women in Trade Unions* by Barbara Drake, 1984, pp. 220 and 221.

Every effort has been made to trace all copyright holders but if any have been inadvertently overlooked the publishers will be pleased to make the necessary arrangement at the first opportunity.

Introduction

One of the most important changes in sociology is currently taking place. It concerns the impact of gender on social analysis. But it is not enough simply to consider women and girls in relation to existing knowledge and perspectives. It is, for example, hard to understand, let alone explain, the position of women in employment without knowing about the circumstances which cause them to sell their labour power under different conditions from men. Similarly, the behaviour of girls may seem inexplicable unless it can be understood as a way of developing strategies to cope with contradictions, change and ambivalence. When, though, the structures and processes are all viewed from a gendered perspective, different aspects of society make sense and tell a continuous story.

This book tries to trace that story, but at present, as Connell notes, 'It is better to accept that the social theory of gender is not a tightly knit logical system. It is, rather, a network of insights and arguments about connections' (Connell, 1985, 261). These insights and connections are the ones this book attempts to explore, but sociology itself has not, in the past, given due consideration to the fact that women inhabit a different 'society' from the largely public and visible one that is usually theorised and researched. It is necessary, therefore, also to use ideas generated by writers outside the subject, and to draw upon the experiences of individual women themselves, both to validate women's experiences and to understand the meanings they attribute to events in order to produce an adequate sociology.

Gender relations involve both men and women, and the structures cannot be understood without reference to both. This book, however, focuses on women themselves as a counterweight to the fact that most of the theories and knowledge we have of society derive from men and their place in the world. Considering women only, at this stage, also enables us to see how different aspects of their lives relate to each other, and a knowledge of this half of the population is necessary before we can properly analyse social relations and social life.

In Chapter 1, biological, psychological and feminist explanations of sex and gender are introduced, and the importance to sociology itself of considering gender relations is illustrated with excerpts from sociologists who reconsider earlier work in the light of current concerns. This raises the problem of how partial our knowledge of social life has actually been and causes us to reconsider even the most basic sociological theories. What would a theory of stratification, for example, look like if it treated women as independent adults rather than 'wives'? Or if it included unpaid as well as paid work in the analysis? Can there, in fact, be a credible theory of stratification that does not attempt to explain gender inequalities?

In the second chapter the lives of women as wives and mothers, the most 'private' of all relationships, are related to social and historical changes and the role of social policy in generating and maintaining these roles and relationships is discussed. Some white feminists have described the family as the single most important structure in maintaining women's oppression, but some black women have claimed that, in a racist society, the family is actually their main source of support. This raises the important, but difficult, issue of the extent to which the explanations that are put forward to explain women's position apply only to particular groups of women. Much more research about the different groups will be needed before we can answer certain questions.

Girls grow up to be women. This process is not necessarily straightforward and unproblematic, as the third chapter illustrates. Learning 'femininity' is a complex process and can only be understood with reference to the 'masculinity' with which it is contrasted. The feminine subcultures, behaviour and stereotypes that are part of girls' lives also figure in their educational experiences. The importance of education in transmitting gender relations is discussed in Chapter 4, where girls' responses to education are also seen in relation to the labour market that girls and women enter. This points to the importance of understanding women's structural position in order to understand girls' behaviour in school – although this behaviour is not described as an unthinking response, rather a negotiated settlement to balance contradictions, desires and possibilities.

To understand women's position in the labour market it is necessary to consider their other responsibilities. Chapter 5 deals with this relationship and maintains that employers are using their assumptions about women's domestic responsibilities and roles to restructure employment to the disadvantage of women. Broad and complex issues regarding the labour market and labour processes have to be explored in order to understand what is happening in this arena and the impact it has on women's lives both inside and outside employment.

The stereotypes of women portrayed in the media have received some attention, but in Chapter 6 the purposes of social stereotypes themselves are considered, as are the 'uses' that women themselves make of the media in order to negate the simple deterministic idea that people are 'influenced' by the media in a straightforward way. If representations of women are common and widespread, women's actual presence in public life is not. Chapter 7 looks at this issue with regard to formal politics and trades unions. Women, though, as you will see, have a long history of organising to protect their rights and some material is presented on this aspect of women's lives.

Women, if largely absent from public affairs, have recently been visible in protest groups outside the formal organisations and in considering the protesters at Greenham Common, in Chapter 8, the ideas concerning 'masculinity' and war are related to the theories of gender differences outlined at the beginning of the book. The Women Against Pit Closures group has been another visible manifestation of protest and is interesting both as a working-class women's group and because it alerts us to the relationships between class and gender.

In order to know more about women, and to produce a better sociology, research has to be done. Having mentioned the theoretical problems, the book concludes with the problems of method. Are there particular difficulties in researching women? Should the research benefit women? Is there such a thing as 'feminist method'? These questions have only relatively recently been discussed but you might wish to review some of the literature on research methods bearing some of these points in mind.

Finally, for examination candidates, it should be stressed that it is not necessary for the words 'women' and 'girls' actually to appear in an exam question in order for you to write about them! They are half the population and an adequate discussion of any topic should take them into account.

Further Reading

S. Ardener, *Defining Females*. Theories about women from many disciplines are assessed and related to the social context in which they have emerged. The book considers ways in which different cultures identify and deal with such 'natural' aspects of women's lives as sexuality and childbearing.

S. Delamont, *The Sociology of Women*. An introduction to the sociological approach to women. It considers the life stages of women and their place in social institutions and processes.

M. Evans (ed.), *The Woman Question*. A huge collection of readings by well-known feminists, covering sexual divisions in the family, employment, politics, education and popular culture. The chapters demonstrate how social processes and institutions operate to maintain and legitimise the differences between women and men.

A. Oakley, *Subject Women*. An interesting book that introduces a wide range of questions with reference to both theories and data.

E. Whitelegg *et al.* (eds), *The Changing Experience of Women*. A collection of essays dealing with the historical separation of home and workplace, the current processes within employment and the domestic sphere, and feminist approaches to the production of knowledge.

1 | Theories of sex and gender

The terms 'sex' and 'gender' are often used interchangeably in everyday life, but in sociological literature they are frequently differentiated. The term 'sex' is applied to differences between men and women that are based on biological differences such as anatomy, physiology, hormones and chromosomes, and in this respect people are *female* or *male*. The term 'gender' is applied to the cultural aspects of male and female roles, in other words the behaviour, personality and other social attributes that are expected of males and females, and these social attributes become the basis of *masculine* and *feminine* roles. The 'correct' gender role in our society also suggests channelling sexuality into heterosexual behaviour, and people who do not conform to this are sometimes labelled as deviant because they infringe common expectations of these roles.

Sexuality and the different capacities of men and women in the reproductive process are particularly likely to be thought of as giving 'natural' reasons for gender divisions in society. If, however, we consider the biological differences, they are not, apart from reproduction, as obvious and clear-cut as might be imagined; for example, girls and boys show no significant difference in size at any age except birth, where boys are slightly heavier, there is no difference in strength for body size, and until puberty the metabolism of females and males is the same. Body changes obviously give women and men different shapes but there is a wide variation from one individual to another. In adults there are some average differences between the sexes – for example men tend to be taller and heavier than women of the same race, society and class – but these are averages: individuals do not necessarily fit the pattern. These averages, though, come to be thought of as 'normal', and are then used to support the idea that this is what should be the case. The first extract by Archer suggests that biological theories purporting to explain the differing roles of men and women in society are themselves influenced by the social arrangements of the time and place. As Connell says, 'that biological difference underpins and explains the supremacy of men over women is the prized belief of enormous numbers of men and a useful excuse for resisting equality' (Connell, 1985, p. 266).

Closely related to the emphasis on biological differences are notions about 'instincts'. The concept of 'maternal instinct' is perhaps the one that is most often used to legitimise women's traditional roles and Oakley, in the second reading, takes issue with this idea, calling it a myth that supports current arrangements. She is not the only writer to take this view – Simone de Beauvoir also pointed out that maternity, which is biologically and seasonally regulated for animals, is arbitrated by society for women and she concluded that the things that identify women 'get their importance from the significance placed upon them . . . and there is no reason to conclude that her ovaries should condemn her to live forever on her knees' (De Beauvoir, 1953, p. 683).

Thus, gender does not follow automatically from biological sex although it is based on biological difference. The social categories of gender are unlike some other categories of social analysis, such as class, inasmuch as they are visibly attached to biological differences, so it is always easy to fall back on biological explanations to account for any gender pattern. Gender has, though, to be worked out and worked towards and Fransella and Frost discuss the social dimensions of the differences in the third reading.

Alternative explanations for gender differentiation have been given by feminist theorists. The excerpt by Banks distinguishes between different kinds of feminist theory, but in practice it is not easy to categorise particular writers. There is also a difference between theory and practice. For example, 'liberal feminists' may believe that gender roles can be redefined if stereotypes are broken down and policies introduced to increase equal opportunities, while 'radical feminists' may see male oppression and power as the problem, requiring more than piecemeal reform. But in practice, feminists of all persuasions would support changes that might improve women's position, even if they have different theoretical explanations for the causes of inequality. The most famous phrase of the radical feminists – 'the personal is political' – is exemplified in the short extract from Firestone: she sees love between women and men as socially and publicly important because women's love has supported men's public achievements, but this is 'work' for which women themselves have had no public recognition.

Sociology itself has been 'gender blind', and in focusing on public, official, dramatic or visible events or people it has often neglected the investigation and explanation of other events and people. Some sociologists have recently begun to reconsider earlier work, including their own, in the light of feminist criticisms, and the extract from Brown discusses how the failure of industrial studies to take gender into account meant that important dimensions of the issues were omitted. Morgan, in the last reading, sees the inclusion of gender as a 'scholarly requirement' necessary to produce adequate sociological explanations at all levels.

Attempts within sociology to explain gender relations have thrown up theoretical problems and a great deal of debate. The most obvious area of contention is perhaps stratification theory, where it seems increasingly unsatisfactory to analyse class in terms of families and households where everyone in the group takes the position of the 'head' at certain times, when at other times (for instance after separation, divorce or death of a partner) they may have a class position in their own right.

The term gender refers to both women and men and to the social processes shaping their expectations and interactions.

☐ Biological Explanations

Biological explanations have been used to justify whatever particular social arrangements exist at any one time, but these can be opposing conditions in different societies. In this sense some biological theories are more context-bound than their apparent 'scientific nature' would suggest.

Reading 1

In one of the New Guinea tribes referred to in Margaret Mead's famous study sex roles were described as being largely the reverse of those found in modern western societies, with the women being the dominant partner and manager of business. The men were described as more dependent than, and submissive to, the women, and more responsive to the feelings of the children than were the women. What is particularly interesting for the present discussion is that the members of this tribe regarded these sex roles as 'biologically natural'. Many societies have ideas of this type to justify their particular sex-role arrangements. Whether the ideas are religious or scientific, and whether we would accept or dismiss their factual content, they all serve the same purpose – to justify the status quo; in other words, to equate 'what is' with 'what ought to be'. . . .

Since the time of Charles Darwin, the notion of an evolutionary plan has gradually come to eclipse that of a divine plan as an argument used to justify the preservation of traditional arrangements in society. In the nineteenth century, Darwin's ideas were used as a basis for arguments linking brain size with the supposedly lower intelligence of women. Even Darwin himself viewed the evolution of mental and physical differences between the sexes in a way that was strongly influenced by the ideas of Victorian society. He remarked that, intellectually, men attain higher excellence in whatever they take up, whether this requires deep thought, reason, imagination or skill with the hands. Darwin viewed the evolutionary origins of this intellectual superiority in terms of men always having had to provide for and defend their womenfolk. Modern anthropological studies of surviving hunter-gatherers indicate that this is an unrealistic view of the economic role of women in prehistoric societies.

This last example in particular illustrates the dependence of particular biological explanations of sex roles on the wider attitudes of the society from which they arose, and the preceding discussion showed how such explanations may be used to justify conservative views of sex roles, in a manner almost identical to the use of religious arguments. Crook made the general point that biological explanations may provide a substitute for the ethical code, lost when religious beliefs are no longer followed, and he suggested that this is particularly likely to be the case in a society (such as our own) where there are many conflicting standards and norms of social behaviour. It is therefore reassuring for many people to believe that their own particular norm, although perhaps considered old-fashioned by some members of society, is nevertheless the one which is consistent with the 'natural order'.

J. Archer, 'Biological explanations of sex-role stereotypes', in J. Chetwynd and O. Hartnett, *The Sex Role System*, pp. 7–8.

Questions

1. Briefly outline the main argument of this passage.
2. List the main 'biological differences' that may be used to support current gender roles in modern society.
3. Take the items on your list and consider, for each one:
   (a) whether you think the difference exists for all men and all women, and
   (b) how the differences are used to explain or maintain any particular gender divisions, e.g. at work, at home, in education etc.

☐ Psychological Explanations

Freudian psychoanalytic theory, as one example of a psychological approach to gender differences, is here explained and criticised. Motherhood, according to Freud, is necessary for the wellbeing of the woman; but Oakley considers this to be a culture-bound explanation. She also maintains that there is no such thing as the 'maternal instinct' in the inborn sense in which it is used. This view might be regarded as contentious by some psychologists, and you might also want to disagree with some of the points.

Reading 2

There are three basic elements of the Freudian position: the identification of the maternal role as an essential component of the feminine gender role; the classification of reproductive behaviour (motherhood) as merely one branch of psychosexual behaviour (femininity); the generalization of penis envy as universal in all 'normal' women, and thus the generalization of the desire and the need for motherhood as a normal feminine attribute. Motherhood is the practical resolution to penis envy. The desire for a (preferably male) child replaces the desire for the male organ. . . .

It follows from these premises that the woman who chooses not to become a mother cannot be a 'feminine' woman: along with motherhood, she rejects womanhood. The choice is cast as a choice between alternative gender roles; to be feminine means to be, or to want to be, a mother: to reject motherhood means to be masculine. . . .

Far from being outdated, this view is a common component of the feminine image today. To have children but turn over their rearing to someone else − even their father − brings social disapproval: a mother who does this must be 'hard', 'unloving', and of course 'unfeminine'. A woman who does not have children is pitied. If her childlessness is willed, she is seen as deviant, abnormal. . . .

Psychoanalytic theory may foster an understanding of why women behave as they do in our culture, but its perspective is culture-bound. Not all cultures insist that women's main vocation is motherhood. Not all females everywhere are subject to the same processes of gender-role socialization as they are in the Western nuclear family. Many make parenthood a somewhat subsidiary vocation for both men and women. . . .

In other words, the function of psychoanalytic theory, so far as the myth of motherhood is concerned, is to keep women in their place – with their children – secure in the pseudo-knowledge that they are doing what it is in their natures to do, convinced that their desire for motherhood is self-constructed and self-fulfilling, rather than, as it actually is, a convenience to their culture, and an inconvenience to them. . . .

There is no such thing as the maternal instinct. There is no biologically based drive which propels women into childbearing or forces them to become childrearers once the children are there.

Nevertheless the 'maternal instinct' is a phenomenon of established popularity today. It is suggested that all women have this instinct, and asserted confidently that all mothers must have it. Irreparable damage to maternal mental health is claimed to follow from a situation in which a woman gives birth to a child and then hands over its rearing to someone else. Childcare by the biological mother is said to be necessary for the sake of the woman's 'own awakened motherliness' as well as for the newborn's needs. . . .

The desire for motherhood is culturally induced, and the ability to mother is learnt. . . .

'Mothering' is not a mystical quality. The expression of love in a warm, caring relationship is its most essential ingredient.

A. Oakley, *Housewife*, pp. 188–203.

Questions

1. Summarise, in your own words, the basic ideas of Freudian (psychoanalytic) theory.
2. What are Oakley's criticisms of the theory? How valid do you consider these criticisms to be? Give reasons for your answer.
3. If 'mothering is not a mystical quality', what is it, according to the writer? Indicate the position you take and give reasons for your answer.

☐ Social Definitions

The fact that there are, in any society, some fixed ideas about the position and capabilities of women and men can be explained with reference to the social expectations that help to regulate social life. The assumptions about people's attributes and appropriate ways of behaving are accepted by many people as 'normal', and it may be easier to accept these than to step outside the taken-for-granted framework and consider other possibilities. This social approach is obviously very different from the biological and psychoanalytic approaches previously mentioned.

Reading 3

Our ideas about ourselves do not simply reflect self-observation. We organize, interpret, and reinterpret what we find ourselves doing, on the basis of notions we already have of what we are about. For one woman a paid job is proof of her independence; for another it is evidence that she is a good wife and mother, who can support her family; yet another might see it simply as her husband's failure to provide as he should.

These basic notions are not constructed from thin air. In every social group there are systems of beliefs, more or less shared, about the nature and appropriate behaviour of women and men. People organize their actions in the light of their knowledge of 'how things are done'; of what they can expect of others; and of what others expect of them. If there were no agreement about these matters social life would be impossible. Life itself would become chaotic and incomprehensible. For it is partly through interaction with others and through common understandings, that individuals are able to plan and interpret their own thoughts and actions.

Some of these common understandings are explicit, external 'rules' imposed from the outside. However, a great many are simply common assumptions that people make about how things should be done. They may not feel like assumptions or beliefs at all. Rather, they may feel like 'facts of life' which do not change and are not questioned. It is a fact of life that 'Women are like this. Men are like that'; 'This is what women do. This is what men do'. Individuals who live according to these beliefs do NOT feel that they are imposed on them, nor do they feel that they are alien – at least for a good deal of the time. The beliefs become a part of them. That is, they ascribe to themselves the qualities of the group to which they see they belong; they want to do what is expected of them; and they value the socially recognized goals.

When people do this, it is not because they are 'conditioned' or 'brainwashed' or 'conformist' or whatever. It is because, *within a particular social framework*, it is the rational thing to do. It makes sense. So long as society is organized according to a particular set of beliefs, and so long as most people act vaguely in accordance with them, it would be exceedingly difficult to see things in any other way and even more difficult to act differently. For to change such basic ways of looking at things would mean changing the structure of society. It would be particularly difficult for any single individual to contravene the rules, in isolation. . . .

One of the things that prevents women from seeing new possibilities is that many of the basic assumptions that people make about women's roles are not explicitly verbalized. Some are of course. For example, there is a much publicized debate as to whether mothers should work, and how old their children should be when they do. Some questions, on the other hand, are never asked even by research workers. Where is the questionnaire which asks whether it is right for fathers of young children to work, or whether they should have shorter working hours to allow them time to take half-shares in housework and childcare? The answers to questions about what women 'ought' to do, depend partly on assumptions which are not stated.

F. Fransella and K. Frost, *On Being a Woman*, pp. 13–15.

Questions

1. 'In every social group there are systems of beliefs, more or less shared, about the nature and appropriate behaviour of women and men.'
   List the shared beliefs about appropriate female and male behaviour as you think they exist in:
   (a) your household
   (b) your school/college
   (c) your friendship group
   (d) television programmes and films that you watch.
2. Compare your list with other people's. Does the gender, age or background of the list-writer make a difference?
3. The authors give an example of a question that is never asked (should fathers of young children work?). Think of some other examples of unasked questions that do not occur to people because certain ways of behaving are 'taken for granted'.
4. 'One of the things that prevents women from seeing new possibilities is that many of the basic assumptions that people make about women's roles are not explicitly verbalized.' Explain and discuss.

☐ Feminist Explanations

The previous passage encouraged us to think of the social definitions and expectations regarding female and male roles and mas-

culine and feminine attributes. Feminist theorists, however, attempt to explain the power relations behind the circumstances that exist. In this passage Banks distinguishes between marxist and radical feminists, and at the end of the passage she mentions 'equal rights feminists'. This latter group are sometimes called liberal feminists and this term is usually applied to those groups or individuals who attempt to change policy and practice enabling women to have more equality. As mentioned in the introduction, other groups of feminists might support these moves but disagree as to how much difference it would make if the sources of power and other arrangements remain unchanged.

Reading 4

Ideologically, radical feminism has no single doctrine and no simple set of goals or aims. Indeed its opposition to organization, and its respect for spontaneity and self-expression, meant not only that each group developed its own programme, but that there were constant splits as groups divided on issues of both ideology and strategy. On the whole, however, the movement is united in its opposition to what it sees as patriarchy or women's oppression by man – a concept that, in its implications, is far wider and more radical than the equal rights concept of feminism. Much of the energy of the feminists, and especially of the feminist intellectuals, has therefore gone not simply into action, or even propaganda, but into a search for the *source* of man's power over women; one of the main lines of division is to be found in the alternative answers that individuals and groups have provided to this crucial question.

The marxist feminists, who represent one kind of answer, try to retain their loyalty to both socialism and feminism. Consequently they continue to give priority to issues of class, although they no longer see feminism, as do many orthodox socialists both male and female, as a necessary consequence of a socialist victory. They are agreed, however, that feminism without socialism is impossible and for this reason, if for no other, the struggle for socialism is given pride of place. At the same time, those women who wish to maintain the link between feminism and socialism find that they can only do so by what amounts to a very radical critique of orthodox marxist views on the position of women.

Radical feminists, on the other hand, see sex as a form of oppression independent of social class. Indeed patriarchy, the oppression of women by men, is seen as not only pre-dating capitalism but continuing after capitalism itself has been superseded. Consequently man himself becomes the exploiter and women the major oppressed class. . . .

One of the most original of the radical feminists to arise in the early days of the American movement was Shulamith Firestone. She based women's oppression in the very fact of reproduction itself, and saw no answer to the problem until artificial childbearing was technologically a possibility. This would enable the family as we know it to disappear, although Firestone, unlike some later feminists, did not propose that men and women should no longer live together. Only by thus breaking the tie between women and reproduction, Firestone argued, can women achieve both economic independence and sexual freedom. Moreover, because the cultural division between the male and female is also based on biological reproduction, artificial reproduction would allow such distinctions to be broken down and men and women to share in characteristics hitherto sharply sex linked. . . .

(Her) critics have pointed out that artificial reproduction could still be used to continue and even enhance male domination unless women were able to control the manner of its introduction. Nevertheless, Firestone's analysis is important because it stresses precisely those aspects of women's position that are crucial in the ideology of radical feminism. The emphasis she lays on women's reproductive functions, and the part played by marriage and the family in the oppression of women, have been and to a large extent remain central to the women's liberation movement both in the United States and elsewhere. Radical feminists therefore, quite unlike the equal rights feminists, have tended to concentrate on the 'traditional female concerns of love, sex and children', even if they have been concerned about them in a very untraditional way.

O. Banks, *Faces of Feminism*, pp. 227–9.

Questions

1. Outline, in your own words, how (a) marxist feminists and (b) radical feminists explain the position of women.
2. Define 'patriarchy'.
3. List any policy or practice changes that you think have been brought about by 'equal rights feminists'. Do you think they have contributed to equality?
4. Why have radical feminists concentrated on 'love, sex and children'?

☐ The Personal
is Political

Shulamith Firestone, who was mentioned in the last extract, is one of the most famous radical feminists, and a short passage of hers is included here to illustrate the way in which she related personal 'feelings' to wider social organisation. This is quite an angry piece and you may feel that in talking about 'public' culture it is dealing with a small portion of life that has included very few men or women. But her view could be applied more broadly to include the emotional 'work' that women do behind the scenes to support more public activities by others. See what you think.

Reading 5

The tired question 'What were women doing while men created masterpieces?' deserves more than the obvious reply: women were barred from culture, exploited in their role of mother. Or its reverse: women had no need for paintings since they created children. Love is tied to culture in much deeper ways than that. Men were thinking, writing, and creating, because women were pouring their energy into those men; women are not creating culture because they are pre-occupied with love.

That women live for love and men for work is a truism. Freud was the first to attempt to ground this dichotomy in the individual psyche: the male child, sexually rejected by the first person in his attention, his mother, 'sublimates' his 'libido' – his reservoir of sexual (life) ener-gies – into long-term projects, in the hope of gaining love in a more generalized form; thus he displaces his need for love into a need for recognition. This process does not occur as much in the female: most women never stop seeking direct warmth and approval.

There is also much truth in the clichés that 'behind every man there is a woman', and that 'women are the power behind [read: voltage in] the throne'. (Male) Culture was built on the love of women, and at their expense. Women provided the substance of those male masterpieces; and for millennia they have done the work, and suffered the costs, of one-way emotional relationships the benefits of which went to men and to the work of men. So if women are a parasitical class living off, and at the margins of, the male economy, the reverse too is true: *(male) culture is parasitical, feeding on the emotional strength of women without reciprocity.*

S. Firestone, *The Dialectic of Sex*, pp. 121–2.

Questions

1. How does Firestone relate the personal emotion of love to wider culture?
2. Do you agree with her view that 'men displace the need for love into a need for recognition' and that 'most women never stop seeking direct warmth and approval'? Illustrate your answer with specific examples from society.
3. Compare Firestone's view of love with the views portrayed in popular fiction, magazines and film. Give particular examples to illustrate your answer.

☐ Rethinking Sociology

The masculine bias of sociology itself led, in the past, to research on public and visible activities associated with the areas of life in which men predominated. Even when women were present this was not necessarily seen as significant, and here Brown discusses the work in industrial sociology and points out that in the most famous study of all – the Hawthorne Experiments – it was a crucial omission. Find out about the Hawthorne Experiments if you do not know about them.

Reading 6

In the literature of industrial sociology there are a large number of studies which make no mention of women as employees for the very obvious reason that virtually no women work in the industry in question. This includes many of the industries which have attracted a lot of attention from social scientists for one reason or another: their propensity to strikes; the rate of technical, organizational and/or market change; unusual conditions of work; the existence of large (and perhaps more accessible to research) plants and firms; or some other circumstances making employment in them more problematic than elsewhere. Thus studies of coal mining, fishermen, dockworkers, lorry drivers, printers, steelworkers, navvies, process workers, seafarers, affluent workers and shipbuilding workers to name but a few – can throw no light on the expectations and actions of women as employees. At the most researchers in such situations have extended the scope of their study to consider the implications of work for family and community life, and vice versa. They have not acknowledged that the absence of women in many cases is due not to the nature of the work but to either the tight control of the labour market exercised by men through their unions, and/or the policies of employers. For example, women worked successfully at many jobs in shipbuilding during the Second World War in this country and in the USA, but were excluded from all production work afterwards. It may seem rather unfair to complain about the lack of such a reference when the dominance of men in such industries is so widely taken for granted, but as is the case with respect to some other aspects of the context of the employment relationship, questioning the taken-for-granted is essential for a more adequate analysis.

However excusable the neglect of women as employees may be in these cases, one must be more doubtful about the way in which some social scientists have tried to provide a general account of certain social processes in industrial situations and have apparently assumed implicitly that it would be valid for situations in which either sex were employed. . . .

In some ways the failure to pay attention to the significance of sexual divisions in industry is particularly surprising in the case of the Hawthorne Experiments, because of the striking contrast between the findings of the Relay Assembly Test Room group of experiments and those of the Bank Wiring Observation Room. In the former situations all the employees were women and as a consequence of the changes, intended and/or unintended, introduced by the investigators these workers increased their output, at least temporarily, and gave evidence of increasingly cooperative attitudes towards management. In the Bank Wiring Observation Room a cohesive work group of men 'restricted' their output, contrary to management's intentions and interests, and the investigators appear to conclude that there was very little the supervisor or anyone else could do about it. Yet the significance of the relay assemblers being women (who in addition had a male supervisor in the test room) and the wiremen being men is not discussed.

This is despite the fairly full discussion of the personal background of many of the employees in question; and despite the authors' clear comments on differences between male and female attitudes as expressed in the interviewing programme.

R. Brown, 'Women as employees: some comments on research in industrial sociology', in D. Barker and S. Allen (eds), *Dependence and Exploitation in Work and Marriage*, pp. 23–5.

Questions

1. Eleven kinds of male workers are listed as having being studied in well known works. List eleven mainly female occupations that could also have been studied. Why weren't they?
2. Studies of miners, lorry drivers and fishermen were carried out in the 1960s. To what extent do you think the men doing each of these jobs depended on women's labour? Give reasons for your answer.
3. In the Hawthorne Experiments the women increased their output after work changes and co-operated with management, while the men restricted theirs. Brown suggests that the gender differences are important to the explanation and should have been explored. How might gender differences have accounted for different responses?

☐ Let's Try Harder

David Morgan did participant observation in a factory department consisting mainly of women and saw gender as a central concern; he considers that for sociology to claim to be explanatory this must always be so. He points out, though, that in doing empirical work male researchers have to be particularly conscious of their gender – which is not to suggest, of course, that all female researchers automatically treat gender divisions adequately. This aspect will be taken up in the last chapter.

Reading 7

My doctoral thesis was based upon a participant observation study of a northern factory. . . . Largely by chance I found myself working in an electrical components assembly department, consisting almost entirely of women. Men were found to be in charge of things, as managers, foremen or chargehands or in some scientific staff capacity or, in one case, as an odd job man. The labour force of assemblers, painters, packers, testers and lower level supervisors were women. . . . the question of gender became a central concern of my thesis. Or rather, the question of women became a central concern, the way in which feminine or domestic identities became realised or significant on the shop floor. . . .

It is worth noting the way in which participant observation contributed to this way of seeing gender as something shaped and patterned in interactional contexts rather than as something unchanging that is brought to every encounter. As a man, I was very conscious of my ambiguous position in the department. My gender placed me – in that context – in the same position as the foreman and managers. The occupational role that I had assumed while carrying out the research, on the other hand placed me in the same position as the female employees. My class – reflected chiefly in my accent and my connections with the university – served to distance me from both categories. Age and marital status were yet further additional factors; some women at least were able to neutralise some of the ambiguities in my status in the department by adopting a quasi-maternal role, expressing concern about how I managed on my own and, in one case, offering to wash my shirts for me. This was not simply a case of a man working among women; it was a case of a man with various other characteristics working in a particular depart-ment – with a particular labour force composition. . . .

The point I want to stress here is that gender differences in fieldwork are not simply a source of difficulties such as exclusion from important central rituals or, in my case, exclusion from all-important interactions in the toilets, but are also a source of knowl-edge about the particular field. The 'participant observer', in short, has a gender identity. . . . 'Taking gender seriously' is not simply a recognition of the justice of the feminist charges against normal sociological practice, perhaps a grudging or a mechanical recogni-tion, but an exploration that can raise new issues and point the way to new solutions. It is, in short, a scholarly requirement, let alone anything else.

Yet it can also be seen that 'taking account of gender' is by no means a simple operation, the addition of one more category of analysis. It means taking account, reflexively, of the gender of the researcher, as well as of the researched, and of the two in interac-tion. It involves, too, a critical examination of the notions of gender differentiation as they enter into sociological analysis, an examina-tion of the routine assumptions that may lie behind the breaking down of numerical data 'by sex'. . . . It involves devising modes of sociological or historical enquiry which may begin to capture the lives of those who are often 'hidden from history' . . . it may be argued that 'taking gender into account' is particularly a problem for male sociologists. . . . The male researcher needs, as it were, a small voice at his shoulder reminding him at each point that he is a man.

D. Morgan, 'Men, masculinity and the process of sociological enquiry', in H. Roberts, *Doing Feminist Research*, pp. 90, 91, 94, 95.

Questions

1. In what ways do you think women's 'feminine or domestic identities' might be realised or attain significance in the workplace?
2. If some of the women in Morgan's study 'neutralised some of his ambiguities' by adopting a quasi-maternal role towards him, what sort of role might men in a male setting adopt towards a female researcher? Give reasons for your answer.
3. Why might it be argued that 'taking gender into account' is particularly a problem for male sociologists?

Essay Questions

1. 'In talking of the division of labour between men and women, we are talking almost exclusively of gender roles rather than sex roles, determined by culture rather than biology.' Discuss. (AEB 1985)
2. 'Sociology cannot claim to be explanatory unless it seriously takes gender differences into account.' Discuss with reference to one particular area of investigation.
3. 'The function of the "myth of the maternal instinct" is to keep women in their place.' Discuss.

Further Reading

A. Oakley, *Subject Women*. Section 2, 'Genes and Gender' is a clear review of the biological and psychological research on sex differences.

R. Frankenberg, 'In the production of their lives men(?) . . . sex and gender in British Community Studies', in D. Barker and S. Allen, *Sexual Division and Society: Process and Change*. Frankenberg discusses the invisibility of women in many well-known sociological studies of communities.

S. Delamont, *The Sociology of Women*. Chapter 2, the sociology of sex and gender, is an interesting and well-referenced discussion of gender typing from birth to womanhood. It also discusses sexuality in relation to dominant ideas.

S. Kessler and W. McKenna, 'Developmental Aspects of Gender', in E. Whitelegg *et al.*, *The Changing Experience of Women*. A discussion and comparison of different kinds of psychological theories, including psychoanalytic, which have attempted to account for gender differences.

2 | The family – wives and mothers

'The family' has been the topic most taken for granted in sociology and the 'ideal type' of nuclear family has often been treated unproblematically. However, the nuclear family is not typical in Britain today as only about 18 per cent of the population live in such households. We should, therefore, speak just of 'families' (Leonard and Hood Williams 1988). Women and children have for centuries been defined in terms of their relationship to the kinship system whilst men have typically been described in terms of their place in the occupational system.

The nineteenth century saw protective factory legislation to reduce female and child labour and also the rise of the notion of the 'family wage' – the idea being that the man was the breadwinner and that his wages should be adequate to support his wife and family. This strengthened men's bargaining position in relation to employers and also made women a cheap pool of labour for casual work. The notion of the family wage and the man as breadwinner also created the position of 'housewife', but not all husbands earned enough, even then, to support their families and many women had to combine very onerous and time-consuming housework and childcare with employment. The ideology of domesticity derived from the family wage is still part of our concept of the family, and the emphasis on the father and husband as the breadwinner was important in the development of ideas of masculinity and femininity. Gittens discusses the importance of these trends earlier this century and the rise of the 'ideology of childhood'.

It was in the nineteenth century that the family thus became defined as a private sphere, although the state intervened, if necessary, to support the emerging ideology. Nowadays very few aspects of state legislation do not impinge on the family – taxation, employment, housing, and education are organised on the assumption of a family unit with the male as the breadwinner. People framing and enforcing laws and policies act on these conventional notions of the family and at a fundamental level the state is involved in actually defining what constitutes a family, a marriage and parenthood. Feminists have argued that the welfare state is organised on the assumption that women and children are,

or should be, dependants of a man. If we considered family
'reality' rather than the ideal type, however, many social policies
would have to be reformulated to take account of the way people
actually live.

The work that is done in the home, mainly by women, is
referred to as *domestic labour*, and feminist writers like Collins
have debated the ways in which this labour is important economically and socially. Domestic labour is also seen as important in
upholding gender relations both inside and outside the home, and
whilst other institutions assume a gender-based division of domestic labour they serve to reinforce and further encourage its
likelihood.

There is an assumption that with more egalitarian ideas and an
increasing proportion of married women employed outside the
home, the domestic load may be more evenly spread than
hitherto. The excerpt by Morris, from her study of redundant steel
workers, shows that this is by no means always the case, even
when men are compelled to be at home; the table from *Social
Trends* illustrates the gap between theory and practice. In other
words, the ideologies of domesticity, masculinity and femininity
have not changed as much as might be supposed, although there
are differences between families, groups and classes. Nor has
increased technology diminished the work as much as might be
assumed: washing machines, for example, led to the demise of
laundries where other people actually did the washing and ironing.
The possession of appliances, too, often means that women take
over tasks previously done by other members of the family, e.g.
the possession of a dishwasher may mean that the woman now
loads and unloads it whereas previously the washing up may have
been allocated to other members of the household. However, if a
woman chooses not to keep her house clean or to supervise the
children 'adequately' she is in danger of being labelled a 'bad' wife
or mother and the state can intervene. Despite their increased
employment, women still have the prime responsibility for servicing and caring for their families and there is still a great deal of
work involved in this.

Marriage is the institution that extracts this work from women:
the marriage contract is also a work contract, sometimes involving
more than housework and childcare. The extract by Finch points
out that when a woman marries a man she also marries his job, and
his work not only structures her life but might also involve her in
unpaid duties to do with his employment. The balance of power
between husbands and wives usually also extends to the allocation

of money, even though the state assumes that what 'goes in' gets distributed fairly or allocated to the person for whom it was intended.

Ideas about motherhood change, but becoming a mother is still the socially recognised way for a woman to become an adult; the primary status passage for men is not fatherhood but paid employment. When feminists argue that mothering is *socially constructed*, they are attacking the institution rather than the experience – the circumstances in which it is carried out in our society – and the interview in the Sanders and Reed extract illustrates those circumstances. The future generation, as New and David argue, is the concern of society, and mothering is therefore both a public issue and a public responsibility.

Feminist writers, then, have 'opened up' the family and related private events to social features of society; some of them have come to see the family and marriage as the main site of women's oppression. The extract from Barrett and McIntosh illustrates this, but recently black writers have argued that the major sites of oppression are not the same for black and white women. The excerpt by Bhavnani and Coulson points out some of the different ways in which the state relates to black families compared with white families, and also makes the point that for black women the family may be the site of resistance to white racism.

□ The Rise of the Housewife

Economic and social changes earlier this century affected both married and unmarried women, particularly in the working class as this excerpt describes. Gittens also discusses the 'ideology of childhood' and the growing emphasis on a clean home environment. Whilst children need to be cared for, clothes cleaned and food provided, you might consider how these needs could have been differently provided for if the role of housewife had not been created.

Reading 1

The structural changes occurring in the socio-economic, political and cultural spheres between 1900 and 1939 significantly altered the relations of all working-class individuals to these systems, albeit in different ways and degrees. These changes in turn led to new meanings and values among the working class, to new interpretations of their situations and, in particular, to the meanings ascribed to the family, work, women, children and family size.

These changes affected everyone in one way or another, but it has been shown that those affecting women were of much greater significance than has often been supposed. Arguably the most important changes were in the economic and occupational spheres. While there was a gradual 'opening-up' of new occupations to women, there was a decline in residential domestic service and an increase in the proportion of women in the clerical, semi-skilled and unskilled sectors. Parallel to this was a decline in the number of married women working and an increase of single women working. This change in the relation of working-class women to the economic system according to marital status was important. As we have seen, it was partly a result of the changing nature of the economy and industry, but was also very much a result of changes in working-class men's relation to the economic system and, in particular, the increasingly widespread assumption that a man's wages should be sufficient to maintain a wife and children as dependants. This concept of the wife and children as dependants was increasingly reinforced by state policies, which had earlier been influenced by middle-class ideologies of domesticity and childhood. . . .

The changing position of children also had important effects on family structure and, in particular, on women within the family. State policy, through the education system, prolonged the period of dependency for children; it also increased the possibility for higher education and individual social mobility for working-class children. These developments, coupled with the dramatic decline in infant mortality, meant not only that working-class parents could assume all their children would reach maturity, but that all their children would be more of an economic liability for a longer period of time than previously. It also put additional pressure on women in particular to be 'good' mothers and to give them a better chance of achieving success.

The development of psychological theories related to the importance of childhood, of medical opinion emphasizing the need for better standards of nutrition, health and hygiene during childhood all contributed to an increasingly elaborate 'ideology of childhood'. Central to this ideology was the concept of a happy, clean home environment; the responsibility for creating and maintaining this environment was invariably seen as the married woman's principal role. The ability to achieve it, however, was directly related to the husband's capacity to earn an adequate and regular wage as well as to the couple's ability to control childbearing. A large family both weakened the economic basis and put too many demands on time and space for the mother. Implicit in both ideologies of childhood and domesticity was the importance of a small family.

D. Gittens, *Fair Sex: Family Size and Social Structure 1900–39*, pp. 181–3.

Questions

1. Describe and discuss the structural changes in the early twentieth century that led to the 'rise of the housewife'.
2. What is meant by
   (a) ideology
   (b) the ideology of domesticity?
   Which aspects of men's employment were necessary to support the ideology of domesticity?
3. Explain the 'ideology of childhood' and the ideas behind it.

□ Domestic Labour

This extract defines domestic labour and explains how it links the family to the economic system. This form of unpaid work has been described as crucial to capitalism, so you ought to consider whether it also occurs in non-capitalist societies. This complicates the issue but it is the basis of an academic debate.

Reading 2

Domestic labour incorporates housework, related activities which produce utilities, childcare and more generalised care for family members. In the broadest sense, the different components of domestic labour are structured by the biological and culturally de-fined needs of families. They further derive from traditional patterns of domesticity; they include the adaptation of scientific knowledge to pre-existing domestic practices and complex domestic rituals, linked to cultural perceptions about what homes should be like. The caring component of domestic labour stems from physiological needs of families, socially accepted 'caring' practices and an ideol-ogy of care. Domestic labour performed in particular families is more narrowly conditioned by family size, stage in the family life-cycle, type and location of home, income and resources.

When domestic labour takes place, a link is forged between families and the economic system. On the one hand, families help to perpetuate the process of capitalist production by consuming goods manufactured in the industrial sector. On the other hand, the utilities produced by domestic labour (such as meals, clean clothes, a comfortable environment and so on) renew labour power through the process of consumption. Caring, in the form of child socialisation, also plays a part in preparing children for their future role in the economy. In producing labour power, domestic labour is an aspect of social reproduction – the 'process by which all the main production relations in society are constantly reproduced and perpetuated'. Indeed, it has been suggested that domestic labour is beneficial and necessary to capitalism. Throughout the 1970s, in what came to be known as the Domestic Labour Debate, a range of arguments were presented showing how domestic labour is of 'the utmost productive importance to capitalism'.

R. Collins, 'Horses for Courses', in P. Close and R. Collins, *Family and Economy in Modern Britain*, p. 64.

Questions

1. What is domestic labour?
2. In which *three ways* is domestic labour said to link the family to the economic structure?
3. If 'domestic labour' is of the utmost importance to capitalism, does it only exist in capitalist societies? Give reasons for your answer.
4. Why is domestic work usually allocated to women?
5. 'When domestic labour takes place a link is forged between families and the economic system.' Explain and discuss.

☐ More Equal Relations

The division of labour within a household is often taken to be 'natural' inasmuch as not only do most of the tasks fall to women, as wives, but they also are expected to take responsibility for organising the household work of other members of the family. It might be thought that there is a more equal sharing nowadays, but paradoxically even if the man is forced to be at home all day his response may be to emphasise his traditional role.

Reading 3

Mr and Mrs D have three children, aged six, eight and ten, and live on a large council estate close to Mrs D's mother. Mr D's parents live on the same estate but rather farther away. After his redundancy Mr D experienced ten months of unbroken unemployment. His wife had taken on an evening job as a factory cleaner about a year prior to her husband's redundancy. Despite the fact that her husband's benefit was reduced because of her working Mrs D decided to keep her job, on the assumption that he would eventually find work (as he did). Later, the couple jointly decided that Mrs D should take on an additional part-time job as a home help. . . . During the period in which Mrs D held two jobs and Mr D remained unemployed Mrs D worked mornings until about 2 pm, and evenings from 5 pm until 8 pm. The children had their midday meal at school and Mrs D would prepare their tea before leaving for work at 4.45 pm, leaving the dishes for her husband. She would then return from work to cook an evening meal for herself and Mr D.

Although in theory Mr D took on the task of keeping the house clean, Mrs D was far from satisfied with the arrangement:

> He doesn't like housework anyway. I suppose he thinks it's not manly. He'd dust and tidy downstairs but he won't do upstairs because no-one sees it, and he won't clean the front windows in case the neighbours see him. I don't mind housework myself as long as I've got the time to do it, but I get irritable at the weekend when there's a backlog of things to do and he won't help. He just tells me to leave it. He doesn't understand that it's got to be done sometime. A full-time job would have been just impossible, but I think we'd have driven each other mad if one of us hadn't been out of the house for a bit in the day.

The couple shopped together while Mr D was out of work, a change from the previous pattern, because Mr D was available to drive his wife to the cheaper shops: 'I'd try to get him to come round the shelves with me and I was glad of the chance to show him the prices. I try to tell him now they've gone up but it doesn't sink in.' Nevertheless, Mrs D had total responsibility for budgeting and for planning and catering for the household's weekly needs.

In principle Mr D is against the idea that a woman might permanently become the main wage earner, while her husband runs the home:

> A 'housewife' means just that. She's supposed to stay at home . . . While I was out of work I felt I wasn't playing a part in things, ashamed that I wasn't keeping my family. I suppose tension would have been worse if the wife hadn't been working, but I'd spend sleepless nights. I'd get up and come downstairs sometimes, at three in the morning, worrying that I'm the man and it's my job to see that everything's right between these four walls. If it's not then it's my fault.

L. Morris, 'Renegotiation of the domestic division of labour in the context of male redundancy', in B. Roberts *et al.*, *New Approaches to Economic Life*, pp. 406–7.

Questions

1. Which household tasks does Mr D regard as 'unmanly' and which tasks is he prepared to do? Why?
2. (a) How did Mr D's unemployment affect his view of himself?
   (b) How did Mr D's unemployment affect Mrs D?
3. Are there any distinctively 'modern' features about this case – that is, things that would have been unlikely fifty years ago? Give reasons for your answer.

□ Who Does What

Of course men, including married men, do household tasks, as this table shows. But it also shows some discrepancy between theory and practice.

Reading 4

See table on p. 29.

Questions

1. The table shows that for married people there is a difference between what people think 'should' happen and what actually happens. Select the discrepancies shown in the table and suggest reasons for their occurrence.
2. (a) Construct a chart showing the tasks that are done in your house-

Household division of labour: by marital status, 1987 (Great Britain, percentages)

	Married people[1]						Never-married people[2]		
---	Actual allocation of tasks			Tasks should be allocated to			Tasks should be allocated to		
	Mainly man	Mainly woman	Shared equally	Mainly man	Mainly woman	Shared equally	Mainly man	Mainly woman	Shared equally
Household tasks (percentage[3] allocation)									
Washing and ironing	2	88	9	–	72	27	–	57	41
Preparation of evening meal	6	77	17	–	55	42	–	42	55
Household cleaning	4	72	23	1	45	52	1	35	62
Household shopping	7	50	43	1	33	65	–	22	77
Evening dishes	22	39	36	11	18	69	9	14	74
Organisation of household money and bills	32	38	30	22	14	62	24	15	59
Repairs of household equipment	82	6	8	74	1	23	64	–	34
Child-rearing (percentage[3] allocation)									
Looks after the children when they are sick	2	67	30	–	47	51	–	40	58
Teaches the children discipline	13	19	67	10	5	83	17	2	80

[1]983 married respondents, except for the questions on actual allocation of child-rearing tasks which were answered by 421 respondents with children under 16.
[2]234 never-married respondents. The table excludes results of the formerly married (widowed, divorced, or separated) respondents.
[3]'Don't knows' and non-response to the question mean that some categories do not sum to 100 per cent.

British Social Attitudes: The Fifth Report. Edited by Roger Jowell, Sharon Witherspoon and Lindsay Brook, Gower, 1988

hold (i) every day (ii) once a week (iii) less often than once a week.
   (b) Note which member of the household does which tasks and who takes responsibility for making sure they are done.
3. Identify different kinds of households, e.g. with more or fewer adults or children, and consider, for each kind of household, whether the work is likely to be allocated differently.

□ Two Marriages – Hers and His

It has been mentioned that the marriage contract is also a work contract – with a wife taking on even more than she bargained for in marrying a man in certain jobs. Marrying a clergyman, doctor, fisherman or soldier, for example, may have significantly different consequences for a woman than had she married a shop assistant, industrial manager or teacher. It should be remembered that, for some women, 'investment' in a marriage may give better economic 'returns' given their alternative employment prospects, although marriage is not as secure an investment as it once was.

Reading 5

There is a familiar theme in our culture that marriage entails 'taking on' your partner, for better or worse. Marriage is not simply a limited liability contract, but each partner – the theme runs – brings to the marriage their total persona and its consequences, which the other has to respond to, handle and deal with. One feature which has to be taken on board is the spouse's job and its implications. What does it mean to marry a bus driver, a solicitor, or a bank clerk, and is that different from marrying a policeman, a clergyman, or a miner? If so, *how* is it different? The examples are chosen advisedly to indicate male occupations, in the belief that this, like so many other features of marriage, is different for men and women: the implications which a man's paid work has for his wife are more significant and far reaching than vice versa. . . . When a woman marries, she marries not only a man but also she marries his job, and from that point onwards will live out her life in the context of the job which she has married. . . .

The structuring effect of a man's work is most clearly visible in the patterns imposed by his working hours. Of course these patterns will be modified by a number of other elements: a wife's own paid employment, having children at school, taking care of an elderly parent, and so on. Each of these in a sense sets its own timetable, and indeed family life can be seen as a series of overlapping and interacting timetables with which wives in particular have to juggle. But the argument here is that a husband's working hours intrude in a special kind of way: in particular, the effects of a husband's working and a wife's working are not symmetrical. In so far as the couple maintain a sexual division of labour, even in a modified form, a wife normally is assigned to 'covering' domestic tasks, especially child care. This leaves her free to pursue other activities, at best, only when he is *not* at work, unless she is able to make alternative arrangements for discharging these responsibilities. . . .

The potential effects of bringing home the *consequences* of work, if not the work itself, are widely recognised in our culture, and the ability of some individuals to 'leave their work behind' at the factory gates or the office door is often much admired. Far more people can bring home work in their heads than bring it in their briefcases, and the possibility that a worker can be mentally 'at work' when overtly engaged in non-work activities presumably occurs in almost any occupation, since he or she may be thinking about features of the work itself, or about aspects of the relationships located in the workplace.

J. Finch, *Married to the Job*, pp. 1, 24, 32.

Questions

1. In some occupations the wife is actually incorporated as an unpaid worker. This may be especially the case if the man works at home. List as many of these jobs as you can think of and describe what the wife is likely to be expected to do.
2. Which jobs have hours and working patterns that make it difficult for other family members to 'timetable' their own activities?
3. In what ways is 'bringing work home' likely to impinge on other family members?

□ Care of the Children

Most people believe children are necessary to turn a couple into a 'family', and married women are subject to a great deal of social pressure in this respect. Whilst childbearing and rearing can be immensely rewarding, the circumstances in which women are

arud
Jane

expected to do it are often difficult and sometimes depressing, as this interview between a young mother and a researcher illustrates.

Reading 6

I was pleased to have the baby, oh yes. It was a bit of an inconvenience, but we'd planned to have one the following year anyway. I was twenty-seven. We were happy about it.

I was a bit upset that I wasn't having her at home, in Australia, but mum came over for two weeks just after she was born. I'm very lucky with my mum – she would and does sacrifice anything for her children. But she had to get back to her job. I was absolutely besotted with my baby, not a moment's resentment that she was stopping me from working. But as soon as mum left I started to feel miserable. It was all right having the baby to look after when she was awake. She was an alert child. But when she was asleep there was nothing to do, just sitting in this two-up two-down place looking at the four walls going bananas, thinking I've got to get out, what am I going to do. I used to go down the road to see my friend and say I just have to get a job, I can't stand it any more. I've since heard that she was quite worried about me. I always thought she was being friendly. I didn't realize she was trying to get me out of myself. I didn't know what the matter was. Then I started to realize what was happening – I'd felt like this before. It was when I was in a flat all one summer with nothing to do after taking my exams, waiting to start articles – I'm a solicitor by profession – my brain stopped. I couldn't be bothered to do anything, not even watch television. I knew it was starting again and I got very frightened. It was awful.

All I could see was that I was going to be stuck at home, not knowing anybody and Tony out at work all day. I missed my mum, not for the mothering but because she was good to talk to. So I used to think, 'My God, what am I going to do?' . . . Then Tony's parents came for a month. They are very old and difficult. No sooner had we got rid of them, when my mum and dad arrived. When we met them at Heathrow I remember saying right, before we start, there are a few rules. They looked at me like I'd dropped a ton of bricks. I told them all the things they were and weren't to do. I was all het up – it was ridiculous.

A couple of days later I was hysterical and crying. Mum was very understanding. Although I was really much better I was still in a state. Then when they went home everything fell apart again. . . . There was a definite tension in our marriage because I was so uptight and so often in a bad mood. . . . It's all well and good for people like Penelope Leach to say the answer for mothers at home is drop-in centres or other groups, but it's so hard when you're at home actually to get motivated to be up and out. You get so used to doing nothing. Even to go round to the shops is an effort. The people who most need to get to a drop-in centre are the ones that won't, who can't be bothered.

D. Sanders and J. Reed, *Kitchen Sink, or Swim*, pp. 192–5.

Questions

1. Which aspects of this mother's situation does she find most depressing? Suggest reasons for this situation.
2. Write a similar account of early motherhood
   (a) imagining the woman is unmarried, lives in poor accommodation and has little money
   (b) imagining the woman has domestic help, relatives living nearby and plenty of money.
3. Are there any common problems in the accounts of the women in these different social circumstances? What factors account for the differences?

☐ Private Trouble – Public Issue

When childcare is regarded as a private and individual matter the responsibility falls solely on the parents, often the mother. The 'downside' of family privacy is described in this extract which also points out that official authorities have definite views on what constitutes a 'good' family and parenting.

Reading 7

Mothers think of themselves as working for their own sakes and for the sake of their children. Thus the relative isolation in which they work seems like a consequence of the sort of work it is. This is ironic, since what mothers do is for the whole of society. Parasitic industries like commercial advertising have the appearance of being socially useful, but bringing up children *appears* to be purely private business. Because each mother has *her* house or flat, *her* washing and *her* children, it is difficult for her to realize that she has *working conditions* in common with Pat up the road, and that these working conditions could be changed.

The belief that childcare is purely a private business has definite political effects. It makes it less likely that working people will get together and make demands on behalf of their children, the new generation, and insist on higher standards for them. It fits in with the official view that family problems and family failures can be put down to the inadequacy of particular individual parents.

As things are, inadequate people are not fully entitled to 'family privacy'. This is a right they forgo when they ask for help or are seen to have need of it. Our argument is not that parents should possess their children and the state should never interfere. On the contrary, we want a bigger role for public authority, more 'interference' of a certain kind. The help we want from the state is the sort of preventive help which reduces the *bad* side of family privacy: the isolation of parents, their near-total responsibility and the burden that it brings, and the sexism which makes the mother *the* key parent in the family but a person of low status and little power elsewhere. State intervention into the family at the moment has a clear political aim. It aims to get families to conform as nearly as possible to the model of a male-headed two-parent family with the man as provider and the woman as emotional mainstay and child carer; in other words, to reinforce the divorce of motherhood from power, which is itself the root of much misery and mistreatment of children. . . .

Official policy assumes that 'good parenting skills' are found in intact, white, middle-class, two-parent family households. Two parents who stay together are assumed to provide better care than one. Ideally this should be true. Yet many women who leave their husbands do so partly because of their husbands' violence to them and/or their children. In these cases the formation of one-parent families may prevent child abuse. . . . Many fathers, not always willingly, see and know little of their children. And the fact that lone parent families are on average poorer than two-parent families tells us nothing about the distribution of resources *within* male-headed households. The income and other resources coming into a family are not shared out fairly between family members. The wife and mother without earnings is particularly vulnerable. She and the children may experience considerable poverty, although her husband is actually earning enough to support them.

C. New and M. David, *For the Children's Sake*, pp. 77–9.

Questions

1. 'The belief that childcare is purely a private business has definite political effects.' What are they?
2. Discuss the advantages and disadvantages of 'family privacy'.
3. Which social welfare policies assume that income is fairly divided within the family once it gets there? How else might the policies operate?

☐ Family Oppression or Family Support?

There is no single feminist perspective on the family. Barrett and McIntosh argue that the family is divisive, nurtures family violence, 'tyrannises' women with motherhood and romanticises marriage – the extract below is from their book. Other feminists, though, have been concerned to protect the interests of women and children who live in families. Bhavnani and Coulson, in the second extract, point to the different position of black families and the women within them, so taking issue with some feminist criticisms of the family. What all these writers have done, however, is to challenge the notion of the family as an isolated, private unit.

Reading 8(a)

Marriage is a form that is sanctified by tradition, not justified by rational social debate. The tradition is one that carries with it the whole historical baggage of male power and patriarchal authority. One has only to think of the traditional wedding ceremony, with its symbolic 'giving away' of the bride by her father to her husband. . . .

Marriage, perhaps, represents a contradiction in the conservative confusion of individualism with familism. For if marriage is the basis of the family, then this supposedly individual and freely chosen form has a state instrument at its heart. Those who defend marriage as what people want and need must explain then why it has to be so massively privileged by social policy, taxation, religious endorsement and the accolade of respectability.

The exclusion of outsiders and turning in to the little family group may seem attractive when it works well and when the family does satisfy its members' needs. But the little enclosed group can also be a trap, a prison whose walls and bars are constructed of the ideas of domestic privacy and autonomy. Why is it that when a man is brutally assaulting his wife the police and neighbours – all of us – are so reluctant to intervene? It is thought of as interfering in a private matter. The bond between them is seen as so special that outsiders should not presume to take a stand, even when it is quite clear that what is happening is an extreme form of physical violence. Why is it that the woman in this situation is so reluctant to go to others for help or protection? She often accepts that violence is a normal risk of marriage or that *she* has failed in some way by inviting violence or not managing to stave it off.

M. Barrett and M. McIntosh, *The Anti-Social Family*, pp. 55–6.

Reading 8(b)

The conceptual framework of *The Anti-Social Family* provides the fixed reference point against which modifications and additions are considered in the light of more information about black women. 'Woman' continues to be defined as a universal category and the oppressive and anti-social character of 'the family' is reasserted. . . . If we consider what issues black people have been struggling over during the past five or ten years in Britain, we see that these struggles have revolved around challenging racism, specifically in relation to the state: over deportation and anti-deportation campaigns, and the police. From asking these questions and reviewing these struggles we are drawn to the need for fresh analysis of the relationship between the state and 'the family' and of how this differs for black and white people. This may lead us to an analysis, and some understanding, that the state may have different strategies for each group. . . .

We begin from a recognition that not all family/household forms and ideologies are equal within Britain, nor are they dealt with as equally valid by the state. For example, the state's practices in terms of the ideology of family unity are pretty contradictory in relation to black people. As a consequence of immigration controls and practices, many black families are split up, either permanently or for a large number of years. The state shows no respect for the principles of family unity in these cases. . . . But the state claims to desire 'family unity' for black families in other circumstances. For example, if a marriage of black people born overseas comes to an end, with one partner perhaps moving to their country of origin, the state attempts to remove/deport the rest of the family/household, using the argument that family unity must be upheld. For black people the British state's commitment to 'family unity' is strongest where such unity is outside the United Kingdom. . . .

That many white socialist-feminists ignore racialist attacks on black households is not new. However, in doing so, they also ignore that harassment and racialist attacks from white women and white men, and sometimes white families, can impel a solidarity within black households. Whatever inequalities exist in such households, they are clearly also sites of support for their members. In saying this we are recognizing that black women may have significant issues to face within black households. Struggles over sexuality and against domestic violence, for example, have been important issues for all feminists, including black feminists, and have involved confronting assumptions about domestic relationships. But at the same time the black family is a source of support in the context of harassment and attacks from white people.

K. Bhavnani and M. Coulson, Feminist Review No. 23, pp. 86–8.

Questions

1. What criticisms do Barrett and McIntosh level against marriage and the family?
2. Bhavnani and Coulson argue against universal notions of 'woman' and 'the family'. What do they mean?
3. What are the differences between the relationship of black families to the state compared with white families and the state?
4. In Britain the family may have more positive elements for some black women than white writers suggest. Why?

Essay Questions

1. Examine the view that the concepts of 'joint conjugal roles' and the 'symmetrical family' are of limited usefulness in understanding marriage in contemporary Britain. (AEB November 1983)
2. How have feminist perspectives helped to develop our understanding of the family and marriage?
3. 'The responsibility of women for housework and childcare serves to perpetuate inequality within contemporary marriage.' Discuss. (AEB November 1985)

Further Reading

G. Allen, Family Life. A clear and straightforward book which includes data from many sources and also discussion of divorce, single parent families and the elderly.

J. Burgoyne and D. Clark, *Making a Go of It: A Study of Stepfamilies in Sheffield*. A study of marriage breakdown, divorce and remarriage through personal accounts. Special attention is given to the problem of stepfamilies. The study provides an example of the ways in which public institutions and structures of power designate what we term our 'personal life'.

Sara Delamont, *The Sociology of Women*. The chapter on 'The mother, grandmother and widow: parenthood and old age' covers some aspects that have not had wide discussion.

Diana Leonard and John Hood-Williams, *Families*. Chapter 6 on the relationship between the family and the state is particularly useful.

Diana Gittens, *The Family in Question*. An excellent sociological discussion of all aspects of the family, marriage, childcare and the role of the state. Also includes fascinating historical details.

E. Malos (ed.), *The Politics of Housework*. An excellent collection of seventeen articles on all aspects of the theory, politics and nature of domestic labour.

Ann Oakley, *Housewife*. The title of this book is a little misleading as it actually puts the discussion of women's role in a broad context.

Deidre Sanders and Jane Reed, *Kitchen Sink, or Swim*. Interviews with women from all over Britain about their lives. Interesting and easy to read.

Janet Finch, *Married to the Job*. A wide range of occupations is discussed in relation to their impact on wives. Interesting to read but not oversimplified.

3 Girls growing up

Boys and girls, from babyhood onwards, are left in no doubt as to which gender they are: clothes, toys and even birthday cards are produced and marketed along this division. Different personality attributes and behaviour patterns are encouraged or discouraged both within the household and outside it, as appropriate to their gender. Young boys may be constrained more than young girls in terms of accepted behaviour, as the presence of 'feminine' characteristics in boys is viewed more negatively than when girls exhibit 'masculine' characteristics. There is a fear that boys will develop as sexual 'deviants' if their behaviour is not checked and, in any case, the adoption of the characteristics of a less powerful group is never viewed with equanimity; whereas girls who act in a manner seen as 'boyish' are thought to be simply 'going through a phase'. The extract by Belotti discusses how one behaviour pattern – flirting – is discouraged in boys and encouraged in girls, and how the latter group elicits positive responses by using that behaviour. Parents are usually unaware of the way their behaviour produces gender differences, as they believe they are responding to innate characteristics.

In adolescence young people in groups have been studied by sociologists interested in forms of subcultures (Hall and Jefferson, 1976; Jenkins, 1983). Most of the groups studied have been groups of boys, and studies such as that by Willis show girls either tolerated on the margins of the group or more or less excluded altogether. The subcultures have been shown to be a means of exploring and practising forms of masculinity for the boys involved (Willis, 1977). We know far less about adolescent girls, not only because of the masculine bias in sociology but also because many girls are not as visible in the public arenas and therefore may be more difficult to study.

The public emphasis on the appropriate nature of girls' interests hinges on romanticism. McRobbie analysed *Jackie*, a magazine aimed at young teenage girls, and the themes of competition with other girls, emotional problems and romance are projected as girls' main concerns. This magazine also addresses girls as though they are a homogeneous group with romance, fashion, beauty and pop music being the limits of their concerns. McRobbie describes the ethos of magazines such as this as 'romantic individualism', but girls themselves are always faced with the problem of how far to display femininity and make judgements about its appropriateness in different situations.

Girls' out-of-home activities are more constrained by parents, and it seems that many girls spend a great deal of time at home in preparation for their trips out, so that the activities associated with their appearance become an important 'leisure activity'. The demands of the adolescent female role are time-consuming and expensive but a necessary investment if, for many of them, finding a partner for social and economic security is their best hope under present circumstances.

The romance purveyed by the media towards women and girls hides the problem of sexuality. Female sexuality has always been subject to contradictory myths – that women are seen on the one hand as passive, on the other as subject to insatiable sex drives if left uncontrolled. Lees sees this dichotomy exemplified in the 'slag/drag' distinction which is discussed in the third extract. In her study of girls the avoidance of the labels involved them walking a tightrope where even the girls' own behaviour may not be the cause of the labelling, rather how boys choose to categorise them for other reasons. The notion of 'love' then enters the arena as a way of legitimising sexual feelings and behaviour towards a boy whilst also offering some protection from a bad reputation; hence the importance of 'romantic love' in this context.

The notion of romantic love, however, leads to negative judgements about the arranged marriages which are customary for some groups of the population. Amos discusses the myths inherent in white people's judgements of black customs in this respect, and points out that most white girls also end up marrying people from their own class and locality. The concepts of 'freedom' and 'choice' are therefore problematic.

In order to fulfil the ideal of femininity and to cope with contradictory messages and expectations, girls develop various coping strategies. They may become involved in the subcultural aspects of femininity to the extent that they will break the law to achieve what society seems to be demanding. The extract by Anne Campbell raises the question of the number of girls involved in shoplifting – although this is not to suggest that it is the strategy used by all girls who want to 'look the part'; baby-sitting jobs and other part-time work can also be a means to the same end.

Beatrix Campbell, in the last extract, discusses another strategy, that of becoming a mother, as a way of moving from adolescence to maturity in localities that offer little employment and few opportunities. There may be dispute about the extent to which girls consciously 'choose' this strategy; nevertheless, motherhood does achieve this transition, because for working-class girls alternative adult roles may be limited, especially in times of recession and in regions with few economic opportunities.

□ Learning to be a Girl

Behaviour that is thought of as typically 'feminine' has to be learned, and only has meaning when there is a form of behaviour to counterpoint it, i.e. 'masculine'. An important aspect of the learning process is the response from others that particular behaviour elicits. In this way, people learn to act 'appropriately' within the gender roles. Belotti suggests that breaking down stereotypes is the prime goal, and she might therefore be regarded as a liberal feminist in the sense that her concentration is on individual behaviour and attributes as the key to change. Although all feminists are in favour of breaking down stereotypes, marxist and radical feminists see the stereotypes as a *result* of social structures rather than the *cause* of inequality.

Reading 1

The way the child's body moves, the way he copies others, cries or laughs, is practically identical in both sexes at the age of a year or a little over, but after this, differences begin to occur. At this age, the greater aggression attributed to males is not yet evident. Boys and girls can both be aggressive; but later on the boys' aggression will continue to be directed towards others while the girls' is often directed towards themselves. For example, flirtatiousness at one year and even beyond is common to both sexes. . . . Addressed by someone he is attracted to, but does not know very well, he will hide his face in his mother's shoulder or behind his hands and smile while winking invitingly. He catches the eye of the other person with this alternation of provocative mimicry and ritual movements of flight. In fact, he is exhibiting genuine flirtatiousness. As boys grow older, this kind of behaviour gradually disappears. In girls it persists precisely because of the reactions it receives from adults. The girl's flirtatiousness is solicited and encouraged, since she is seen as being already so 'feminine'. In the case of the boy, his attempts at flirtatiousness are not accepted, and he is taught other patterns of behaviour. It is because adults do not give any positive response to this type of seductiveness and at the same time offer more dry, 'masculine' gestures for the boy to copy that the more effeminate mannerisms gradually disappear in the boy. Girls, on the other hand, continue to use them because they copy them from their mothers and from other women and are encouraged to adopt them by the positive response that they obtain from adults. It is to be noted that girls whose mothers are strict and not given to so-called feminine mannerisms, have a limited and often non-existent repertoire of flirtatious tricks because they have not had much to imitate. The adult's compliance and condescension teach the girl that she gets far more by acting in this way than by stamping her feet in a rage, or by asking for what she wants in a straightforward, dignified way. Thus she learns to say 'I can't do it', 'I don't know how to', 'help me', in such a charming way as to be irresistible. If her acting the part of a weak, incapable creature who is charmingly imploring gives pleasure to the adult, she will do so because she is anxious to live up to expectation and at the same time get what she wants. This is a mechanism which is learned at the earliest age and functions unfailingly. A woman will use it all her life, paying for it with a loss of autonomy and a sense of frustration which such a loss inevitably generates.

Sexual conditioning can only work in one sex on the understanding that the direct opposite will be produced in the other sex. The superiority of one sex is based exclusively on the inferiority and weakness of the other. If the little boy feels himself to be a little man simply on the basis of domination, someone will have to agree to being dominated. But if boys are no longer taught to dominate and girls no longer taught to accept and love domination, unexpected and hitherto unsuspected expressions of individuality may flourish, far richer, more articulate and imaginative than the restricting, humiliating stereotypes.

E. Belotti, *Little Girls*, pp. 54–5.

Questions

1. What 'other patterns of behaviour' might young boys be taught to replace early behaviours regarded as feminine?
2. What does the author mean when she maintains that the effectiveness

of flirtatious and charming behaviour is paid for, by women, with a loss
of autonomy?
3. Do you agree with the author's contention that if boys and girls were
brought up differently 'expressions of individuality' would flourish?
Give reasons for your answer.

□ The Culture
of Romance

One of the striking features of magazines aimed at girls is how
little the message or the presentation has changed over the years.
The characters are not only as stereotyped as you would expect,
but are also without regions or accents and the world impinges
very little on what is presented as the main activity of life – finding
and keeping a partner. The evidence of the magazines seems to
support the view put forward in another context (see extracts 3 and
4 in Chapter 2) that ideas of masculinity and femininity have
changed very little.

Reading 2

The way the figures look, act, and pose contributes also to the
ideology of romance. For a start there is very little variation in types of
physical appearance. . . . *Jackie* boys fall into four categories. First,
there is the fun-loving, grinning, flirtatious boy who is irresistible to all
girls; second, the 'tousled' scatterbrained 'zany' youth who inspires
'maternal' feelings in girls; third, the emotional, shy, sensitive and
even 'arty' type; and fourth, the juvenile delinquent usually portrayed
on his motor bike looking wild, aggressive but 'sexy' and whom the
girl must 'tame'.

In every case the male figure is idealised and romanticised so that
there is a real discrepancy between *Jackie* boys and those boys who
are discussed on the Cathy and Claire page. The central point here
is that *Jackie* boys are as interested in romance as the girls.

'Mm! I wish Santa would bring me that for Christmas . . . so how
do we get together?'

and this, as countless sociological studies, novels and studies of
sexual behaviour indicate, simply does not ring true. Boys in contemporary capitalist society are socialised to be interested in *sex*,

although this does not mean they don't want to find the 'ideal' girl or wife. [. . .]

Female characters, significantly, show even less variation in personality. In fact they can be summarised as three opposite or contrasting types. The 'blonde', quiet, timid, loving and trusting girl who either gets her boy in the end or is tragically abandoned; and the wild, fun-loving 'brunette' (often the blonde's best friend) who will resort to plotting and conniving to get the man she wants. This 'bitch' character is charming and irresistible to men although all women can immediately 'see through' her. Finally, there is the non-character, the friendly, open, fun-loving 'ordinary' girl (who may perhaps be slightly 'scatty' or absent-minded). She is remarkable in being normal and things tend to happen *to* her rather than at her instigation. Frequently she figures in stories focusing round the supernatural. . . .

The messages which these images and stories together produce are limited and unambiguous, and are repeated endlessly over the years. These are (1) the girl has to fight to *get* and *keep* her man, (2) she can *never* trust another woman unless she is old and 'hideous' in which case she doesn't appear in the stories anyway and (3) despite this, romance, and being a girl, are 'fun'.

No story ever ends with *two* girls alone together and enjoying each other's company. Occasionally the flat-mate or best friend appears in a role as 'confidante' but these appearances are rare and by implication unimportant. A happy ending means a happy couple, a sad one – a single girl. Having eliminated the possibility of strong supportive relationships between girls themselves, and between people of different ages, *Jackie* stories must elevate to dizzy heights the supremacy of the heterosexual romantic partnership.

This is, it may be argued, unsurprising and predictable. But these stories do more than this.They cancel out completely the possibility of any relationship other than the romantic one between girl and boy. They make it impossible for any girl to talk to, or think about, a boy in terms other than those of romance.

A. McRobbie in B. Waites, T. Bennett and G. Martin (eds), *Popular Culture: Past and Present*, pp. 272–5.

Questions

1. 'The way the figures look, act and pose contributes to the ideology of romance.'
   (a) What do you understand by this statement?
   (b) Discuss its implications.

2. Acquire some teenage magazines and
   (a) Note how many different male and female stereotypes occur in the stories.
   (b) List the 'messages' that the magazines seem to be portraying.
   (c) Look at the Problem Pages and see whether your evidence supports McRobbie's view that 'real boys' do not bear much relationship to those portrayed in the stories.
3. How influential do you think these magazines are over girls' views of the world? Give reasons for your answer.

□ Sexuality

The world portrayed in magazines may be saturated with romance but in the real world girls have more pressing problems. They risk being stigmatised as either a 'slag' or a 'drag' if their behaviour, appearance or even friendships are not carefully controlled. Girls' sexuality is problematic for both boys and adults and can thereby become a problem for girls themselves until they incorporate it into romantic love – which lends it acceptability. You might also consider this passage in relation to Firestone's contention (see Chapter 1) that love is 'work' for women.

Reading 3

A look at the actual usage of 'slag' reveals a wide variety of situations or aspects of behaviour to which the term can be applied, many of which are not related to a girl's actual sexual behaviour or to any clearly defined notion of 'sleeping around'. A constant sliding occurs between 'slag' as a term of joking, of bitchy abuse, as a threat or as a label. At one moment a girl can be fanciable and the next 'a bit of a slag' or even – the other side of the coin – written off as 'too tight': . . .

This constant sliding means that any girl is always available to the designation 'slag' in any number of ways. Appearance is crucial: by wearing too much make-up, by having your slit skirt too slit; by not combing your hair; wearing jeans to dances or high heels to school; having your trousers too tight or your tops too low – as one girl said, 'sexual clothes'. Is it any wonder that girls have to learn to make fine discriminations about appearances and spend so much time deciding what to wear? . . . Some clothes, however, indicate a lack of sexiness that can lead to a girl being classed as unattractive. . . . Whom you mix with also counts:

I prefer to hang around with someone who's a bit decent. 'Cos I mean if you walk down the street with someone who dresses weird you get a bad reputation yourself. Also if you looked a right state, you'd get a bad reputation. Look at her y'know.

Looking weird often means dressing differently from your own group.

Behaviour towards boys is, of course, the riskiest terrain. You musn't hang around too much waiting for boys to come out (but all girls must hang around sufficiently); talk or be friendly with too many boys; or too many boys too quickly; or even more than one boy in a group; or just find yourself ditched.

Almost everything plays a part in the constant assessment of reputation – including the way you speak. . . . Thus 'slag' can just as easily be applied to a girl who dresses or talks in a certain way or is seen talking to two boys or with someone else's boyfriend. The point is that irrespective of whether, in a particular case, the use of the term 'slag' is applied explicitly to sexual behaviour, since a girl's reputation is defined in terms of her sexuality, all kinds of social behaviour by girls have a potential sexual significance.

There is nothing romantic in the girls' stark, indeed grim appreciation of the state of gender relations and it is here that the term 'slag' is always pivotal. A girl who is dropped is particularly vulnerable.

Sue Lees, *Losing Out: Sexuality and Adolescent Girls*, pp. 36–9.

Questions

1. What are the social behaviours that can result in a girl being labelled in a sexually derogatory way?
2. What factors prevent most girls from ignoring the social restrictions?
3. What purpose does this process of sexual labelling of girls serve for boys?
4. To what extent are the different expectations about girls' and boys' behaviour legitimated by assumptions about biological differences?

☐ 'Choosing' your Partner

The notion of romantic love, as presented in western culture, is not seen as specific to time and place but is taken to be the desirable state of affairs for all people everywhere. This leads to a denigration of other patterns of marriage arrangements.

Reading 4

The practice of arranged marriages is most frequently used as an explanation for the oppression of Asian girls. It is one area which has received frequent sensational news headlines in the papers and many television programmes have been made about it. Most of this coverage has given a distorted and false picture of the tradition and practice of arranged marriages. The overall stereotypical image is that of Asian girls caught between two cultures, her parents' culture and the culture of her white English peers. Asian girls are said to see their white friends at school or work going out to discos and films and 'choosing' their own boyfriends and potential husbands, while they (the poor Asian girls) are forced into a marriage with someone who is usually twice their age, someone who doesn't understand the English romantic etiquette like white men do and, of course, someone whom they have never seen until the actual wedding ceremony. Asian girls are said to have absolutely no 'freedom' to partake in the choosing of their husbands while white English girls have all the 'freedom' they want or need. If Asian girls had the same degree of so-called 'choice' about their marriage then it would help to create a more integrated society. Invariably, it's the parents with their archaic ideas who are seen as stopping this integration into white British society.

The stereotype that we have outlined might seem a little crude, but these are the ideas and attitudes which are dominant amongst most white people.

Nothing, however, could be further from the reality. This kind of gross generalisation has led to many myths about the practice of arranged marriages (we are not denying that arranged marriages are oppressive, but marriage as practised in white British culture is also oppressive).

What we want to challenge is the illusion that white girls have a great deal of choice about whom they marry. The reality is that, in the majority of cases, if they marry they will marry boys from a similar class background, in the same region or geographical area.

For example, what chance does a white working-class girl who has left school at sixteen with a few or no CSEs and is working in a factory or doing a typing course, have of meeting up with and marrying a white middle-class boy who has been to the local grammar school, then university, and is professionally employed? Not only is there not much chance of these two ever marrying, but there's not much chance of them ever even meeting.

So 'choice', 'arrangement' and 'freedom' are all relative concepts and often it is people's class which determines whom they meet, and whom they marry, more than any romantic or idealistic notions of falling in love with 'Mr Right' who happens to fatefully cross your path.

For Asian girls, the amount of choice they have over whom they marry varies a lot from one Asian community to another, and from one Asian family to another. Some parents are more strict than others, just like some white English parents exercise more control over their children than others.

V. Amos and P. Parmar, in A. McRobbie and T. McCabe (eds), *Feminism for Girls*, pp. 140–1.

Questions

1. What, according to the authors, is the stereotypical view of arranged marriages for Asian girls?
2. How do the authors counter this view?
3. Discover the origins and purposes of arranged marriages and discuss the benefits and disadvantages for both women and men compared with the non-arranged variety.

□ Living Up to Expectations

Appearance is an important aspect of 'femininity' as portrayed in our society. Perhaps it would be more accurate to speak of appearances, as women and girls, much more than men and boys, are expected to present themselves differently in different settings. Many girls and women enjoy this and regard it both as a challenge and as fun. It can, however, be a cause of worry and frustration when financial or personal circumstances are inadequate. For young people clothes and appearance are also part of subcultural styles to which adherence is part of belonging.

Reading 5

Teenagers whose style and self-concept have come to depend on buying power and subcultural knowledge of the right thing to buy will be driven to theft when economic circumstances demand it. It is not a simple case of capitalist greed; the issue is consumables as self-definition. . . .

The greater proportion of shoppers are female. This is no less true today than 50 years ago. Girls feel at home in a store, whereas for men it remains an alien environment. . . . Shops encourage customers to pick items up – a half-way step to purchasing. This is particularly true of cosmetics and clothing. Prospective customers are encouraged to 'test' perfumes and skin preparations. Dresses are left on open racks to be picked up, carried around and tried on, with the idea that once it has been worn in the fitting-room the customer will become firmly attached to a dress and buy it. Unattended fitting-rooms and easily accessible goods clearly encourage theft as well as legitimate purchase, but, as previously noted, stores are unwilling to change their layouts, as such a move would deter *bona fide* customers. . . . Possessions exert a twofold influence. First, everyone's choice of possessions makes particular statements about the kind of person he or she is. In the case of subcultures this is fairly easy to see, since style is dictated either by the central London scene or by manufacturers with a stake in the movement. But even for those who do not subscribe to a received style, magazines and advertisements encourage a more classical style or even persuade the reader to develop her own. . . .

The impetus to shoplift, then, is a product of the interaction between self and possessions, between work and fun. Why is it a crime in which girls participate in greater numbers than in any other offence? The answer given by many writers is solely in terms of the greater exposure among women to goods and shops; the simple opportunity thesis. But as well as this, it is important to consider the extent to which self-representation and appearance are particularly important to girls economically and therefore psychologically. . . .

Girls' preoccupation with physical appearance has been inculcated historically, and in each girl's own development, through family, school and the media. Its purpose is not merely to fill up time in a fundamentally pointless existence (*Jackie* magazine: 'When you're all alone you can have a great time making yourself up . . . trying out different hairstyles and seeing what suits you best'), nor is it simply aesthetic. . . . The success at which the girl aims is marriage. Marriage to the right man guarantees economic security for life. Her future financial well-being rests on her looks. She may be a humble typist, but if she is beautiful, she could be married to a millionaire tomorrow. Success stories such as these are carried by the newspapers all the time. . . .

With so many demands on incomes that are often quite low, it is hardly surprising that girls are heavily involved in shoplifting. The pressures – material, psychological, social, romantic – assault them from every side. The shops invite them to touch, smell, feel and wear everything that they need for instant success in all these spheres. When the temptations are all weighed up and the chances of detection calculated, it is remarkable that so few girls do it.

A. Campbell, *Girl Delinquents*, pp. 120–31.

Questions

1. What do you understand by the phrase 'consumables as self-definition'?
2. The author considers that the simple 'opportunity thesis' is not adequate to explain the extent of girls' shoplifting. What explanations does she give?
3. Why are physical appearances so important for girls, according to the author? Do you agree? Give reasons for your answer.

□ One Way of Becoming a Woman

Motherhood can mark the transition to adult status for girls who live in circumstances and areas where the wage-earning transition is not possible. The transition, however, is by no means simple or easy when the mother is a young single parent in poor housing and poverty, as this extract illustrates. The fact that childcare is regarded as private and individual (see Chapter 2) is relevant to the girls' lives, as is the fact that social policies are framed on the basis of the 'conventional family' (see Chapter 1). You should also note the fact that many girls are choosing not to link motherhood with marriage initially, and thus their behaviour is not merely a traditional response in any simple way.

Reading 6

They have no place of their own – either because they can't afford the Ritzy redoubts of the youth culture, or because home is a place where you're in the way. The only place left is the streets, and street life either costs money, or is dangerous. Hard-line street life doesn't sit easily with the girls' culture, and for all their stylish revolt, in the end the only way to belong seems to be part of the community of women. Faced with the alternatives of the dole, or the angry aggravation of the streets, motherhood brings a sense of belonging. More important, it offers a transition from immaturity made permanent by poverty, to a state of maturity. . . . The real change is that many are doing it alone. Men come and go in their lives, but there is no necessary connection between motherhood and marriage. They are going it alone not only because they happened to 'get caught out', but because it is an alternative to aimless adolescence on the dole. 'I always wanted to have a child,' said a nineteen-year-old woman living on a Sunderland housing estate with her parents. Youth unemployment there has reached 50 per cent. 'Having a baby makes me feel a lot older and more mature. At first my mam and dad weren't pleased about me falling pregnant, and they used to go on about how was I going to manage'. . . . One of the women on this Sunderland estate told me they all recognised the drive: 'It's part of becoming a member of the community instead of just a reckless teenager. You don't need to get a job, when you're a mam. When you're a mam somebody *needs* you.' . . .

But it's a road riddled with paradoxes. They are lonely and they are poor. Though if you're young and poor the surest guarantee of a council house is parenthood, only because the housing cataclysm of the fifties and sixties produced cold, damp deserts that no one else wants to live on. The young mothers take up the local authorities' slack stock. . . .

A single mother I met in Sheffield has got housing, but in a Dickensian block of flats, on the fifth floor, with no lift, a damp kitchen, bathroom and hall where the wallpaper seems to stand up only out of inertia because it isn't sticking to the walls. There is no place for the child to play. 'One day a neighbour opposite came to tell me my little boy was hanging over the other side of the railings on our landing. So after that I would never let him out to play, but then a social worker came to complain that I was keeping him in and away from other children.'

B. Campbell, *Wigan Pier Revisited*, pp. 65–8.

Questions

1. 'Motherhood brings a sense of belonging when the alternatives are the dole or hanging around the streets.'
   (a) What do you understand by this statement?
   (b) What does it imply?

2. Consider the reasons why some girls are choosing not to connect motherhood with marriage, at least when they are young.
3. To what extent could the problems that young single mothers and their children face be alleviated by changes in social policies? Why are such changes not occurring?

Essay Questions

1. Comment on the view that sociological knowledge of youth and adolescence is inadequate because of a failure both to study girls and to understand their responses.
2. 'The ways in which boys and girls express their sexuality are socially constructed and socially controlled.' Discuss.
3. Adolescent behaviour is both a reflection of, and a preparation for, adult behaviour. Discuss with reference to gender relations.

Further Reading

C. Griffin, *Typical Girls?* A study of girls that argues there is no such person as a 'typical girl' by looking at their views on all aspects of their lives.

S. Lees, *Losing Out: Sexuality and Adolescent Girls*. A study of girls showing how sexuality impinges on all aspects of their lives using the girls' own words and vivid illustrations of gender relations.

D. Leonard, *Sex and Generation: A Study of Courtship and Weddings*. An interesting examination of the rituals associated with courtship, engagements and weddings.

A. McRobbie and T. McCabe, *Feminism for Girls*. Read the chapter by McRobbie on *Jackie* from which the extract in this chapter was taken. The chapter by Connell *et al.* on Romance and Sexuality is also a relevant critique of dominant myths.

J. Sarsby, *Romantic Love and Society*. A discussion of the historical roots of romantic love and its place in both the past and the present.

S. Sharpe, *'Just Like a Girl': How Girls Learn to be Women*. This popular book looks at the socialising agencies perpetuating gender stereotypes, but also, through its interviews with girls, show the ideas they have.

S. Sharpe, *Falling for Love: Teenage Mothers Talk*. The first book on teenage mothers that allows them to speak for themselves showing, among other things, that they are not unusual teenagers.

4 | Education

The role of education in social and cultural reproduction has received much attention from sociologists, but mainly in terms of social class. Bowles and Gintis, for example, developed a theory of 'correspondence' between class, classroom relations and work in the labour force (Bowles and Gintis, 1976). They saw the reproduction of the social relations of production as partly achieved by their structural equivalent in schools – the system of authority relations that 'prepared' pupils for authority relations outside. There is, however, another set of social relations that may be seen both within and outside education – patriarchal relations, or the authority of men over women.

With regard to education, liberal or 'equal opportunities' feminists have, by and large, concerned themselves with the problem of equal access to male-dominated areas of the curriculum in order to equalise outcomes. Marxist feminists have meanwhile considered not only the class differences between women and girls but also the ways that education reproduces their structural location in terms of other institutions as well, such as the labour market. Radical feminists have paid attention to the nature of the 'knowledge' that is transmitted in education, seeing it as a male-dominated view of the world which is partial but serves to legitimise male power. But this is a crude distinction, because in practice marxists have also considered the 'nature of knowledge'. Radical feminists also see connections between women's position in different institutions, and some liberal feminists have also concerned themselves with the more subtle aspects of schooling besides simply 'access'. This difficulty of placing particular writers or researchers in one category or another was noted in Chapter 1, and some of the excerpts in this chapter also illustrate this point.

It is not accurate to say that girls 'underachieve' at school; at secondary level girls have obtained higher grades than boys, and the gap at 'A' level is no longer very wide. The difference, in achievement terms, lies in the different subject choices that girls and boys make, and this is illustrated in terms of exam passes in the first Reading. Subjects become 'gendered', and in the second excerpt Harding discusses this with regard to science. The most well known action-research project to encourage more girls to do science and technology is the Girls Into Science and Technology (GIST) project and the extract by Whyte describes aspects of that project. This might be described as part of the liberal interventionist movement, but you should note that it was more than an attempt to encourage the girls to do the 'same' science – the subject itself was put under scrutiny.

The nature of the knowledge that is presented is considered further in the reading by Spender, where she concludes that not only is the male view of the world partial but it has also succeeded in rendering women's experiences invisible – to be recreated each generation in the absence of its own history. Education, in these terms, becomes synonymous with male education taught also to females.

Despite exam passes, therefore, we cannot assume that all is well. The jobs girls enter, and the careers they choose, represent a narrow range of possibilities, and if education is about more than simply gaining qualifications girls also receive significantly different experiences in their schooling than do boys. It is at the level of school interaction and culture that feminist researchers have attempted to explore the processes of gender relations that help to explain not only educational achievement but also cultural ideas regarding femininity and masculinity that are reflected, created and modified within schooling.

The nature of coeducation has come under scrutiny by many feminists. Both liberals and radicals see single-sex classes and groups as a way of breaking traditional sex stereotypes, and radicals also consider mixed schools as one of the main means of reproducing patriarchal relations. But single-sex schooling was, historically, the major form of the reproduction of gender relations and coeducation has emerged as a variant, not an alternative, to that form. The extract by Delamont shows that even in a girls' PE class the presence of boys elsewhere is used as a form of control over the girls themselves. Within mixed classrooms the gender relations between girls and boys are intertwined with gender relations between teachers and pupils; the extract by Stanworth illustrates this and also leads us to consider that the requirements of 'femininity' may be at odds with the requirements of showing 'cleverness'; which involves girls in having to decide how, when, where and to what extent they should adopt a feminine role which relates to the discussion in Chapter 3. This emphasis on the actual processes within coeducation does not necessarily mean that all feminists are in favour of single-sex schooling, for a strategy for one sex does not challenge the overall reproduction of gender relations and leaves untouched the problem of boys' education. The question of how best to educate boys to overcome traditional male attitudes is, as yet, unresolved but it is an important question.

It is sometimes assumed that stereotyped sex-role messages, like others, are 'successfully received'. It is important to note, as Anyon (1983) points out, that complete acceptance is actually rather rare. There is, rather, a simultaneous process of accommodation and resistance as girls attempt to cope with contradictory social messages. The official educational ideology, for example, may emphasise achievement and equality but there are also messages about femininity and masculinity and future roles, which may contradict this ideology; these messages also have class and racial dimensions. The extract by Fuller describes how a group of black girls managed some of the contradictions by accepting the legitimacy of the school only in some respects and resisted being 'good' pupils in other respects in order to maintain their identity.

In considering the processes of gender relations within education the notion of girls' 'choices' of subjects and jobs becomes more problematic and complex. The choices owe something to these school processes, the cultures and stereotypes of femininity and masculinity and also the actual opportunities available in the labour market as it is constructed. The reading by Buswell discusses training, at post-school level, for girls in relation to these factors and also the purposes of vocational education historically.

The emphasis on class inequality in the sociology of education has served to obscure the fact that gender (and race) differentials, unlike class differences, can only be eliminated by *group* mobility. Education may sometimes help individuals to change their class but it cannot change gender (or race), and thus the structural position of these groups becomes an important aspect of understanding their educational experiences.

☐ Achievement

The table on p. 56 refers to 'O' level passes, but the patterns are likely to apply to all abilities in GCSE in terms of subject choice.

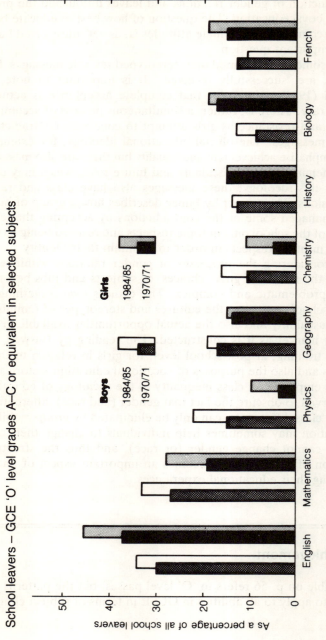

Reading 1

School leavers – GCE 'O' level grades A–C or equivalent in selected subjects

As a percentage of all school leavers

English, Mathematics, Physics, Geography, Chemistry, History, Biology, French

Boys — 1984/85, 1970/71
Girls — 1984/85, 1970/71

[1]Includes grade 1 results in CSE examinations, but excludes 'O' level passes on 'A' papers.

Source: Department of Education and Science: from *Social Trends*, No. 17, 1987.

Questions

1. Which subjects did more girls enter and pass than did boys?
2. Which subjects accounted for almost equal numbers of passes for girls and boys?
3. Which subjects did more boys enter and pass than girls?
4. Do you think GCSE will result in any changes to these patterns? Give reasons for your answer.

☐ The Problems of Science

Girls' underrepresentation in science subjects has been a cause for concern as these are 'high status' subjects which are also a necessary requirement for many jobs. In this extract the author explains why she thinks science has become 'gendered' as male.

Reading 2

In any discussion of girls' achievement in science two factors must be recognized. One, that school subjects (as well as adult occupations) carry a sex bias in terms of the relative numbers of males and females who are involved in them (and this has been shown above to be more extreme in mixed schools). Physical scientists, both teachers and those made visible in the media, are more likely to be men than women; physics textbooks contain many more references to males than to females, and the type of example chosen for discussion is more likely to refer to a traditionally masculine interest than to a feminine one.

The other factor is the vocational role that the sciences have assumed in the school curriculum. In spite of the cultural claims made for science education, the physical sciences have been chosen largely by pupils who wish to use them in future occupations and not by others. There is a sense, also, in which biology (including, as it does, the working of the human body and aspects of hygiene and nutrition) has vocational relevance for girls, preparing them for the home-based role. . . .

One can argue that there are at least two dimensions influencing girls' choice of the sciences and possibly their achievement in them. These are the distribution of school subjects or occupation along a masculine/feminine dimension, and commitment to work outside the home. The first may be constructed from the relative numbers of boys and girls choosing to study each subject or to follow an occupation; but, while the second may be conceptualized, it is more difficult to measure. Its importance is in the increased motivation to succeed that commitment to work confers.

Theoretically, the two dimensions may be placed at right angles to define four cells. Individuals may then be placed within the cells in terms of their position on the work commitment dimension and their involvement in sex-typed activities.

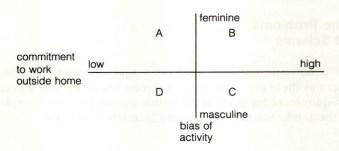

Dimensions relating to the choice of science subjects

J. Harding, in R. Deem, *Schooling for Women's Work*, pp. 94, 95.

Questions

1. What two factors, according to the author, are important to achievement in science?
2. Write a few words describing the 'ideal type' of girl who would, according to the diagram, belong in
   (a) Cell A
   (b) Cell B
   (c) Cell C
   (d) Cell D.

☐ 'Girl friendly' Schooling

Encouraging girls to move into male-dominated areas of the curriculum has been described as part of the liberal or equal opportunities tradition. The following extract describes an action-research attempt to do that, with regard to science and technology, but note that this project had broader aims than simply eliminating the 'deficiencies' of girls.

Reading 3

Girls Into Science and Technology (GIST) was the first major schools-based project addressing problems of sex stereotyping at school, and was an example of 'action research' in education; the project simultaneously took action to improve girls' achievement in science and technology and investigated the reasons for their under-achievement. The project team collaborated with teachers in eight coeducational comprehensive schools in the Greater Manchester area to devise and implement intervention strategies designed to improve girls' attitudes to the physical sciences and technical subjects. . . .

The action-research plan was as follows:

1. We tested children's spatial ability and their science knowledge on entry to secondary school, and explored their attitudes to science and sex roles. The results were then fed back to schools.
2. We worked with teachers to increase their awareness of the impact of gender on educational achievement and outcomes, and to view it as a pedagogical issue.
3. A programme of visits to schools by women working in science and technology was mounted.
4. On the basis of (2) and (3) above, teachers and schools were invited to mount their own interventions; these included development of more 'girl friendly' curriculum materials, single sex clubs and classes, observation to increase awareness of sex differences in classroom interaction.
5. Children's attitudes to science and to sex roles were again measured for comparison with the initial survey, and their subject options monitored and compared with previous year-groups in each school.

. . . GIST had more success in altering children's attitudes than their subject choices, suggesting that it is easier to change attitudes and beliefs than actual behaviour. Pupils in action schools became markedly less stereotyped than pupils in control schools. They also had slightly more positive attitudes towards science and scientists and were less likely to define them as exclusively masculine. . . . During the project there was a shift away from locating the issue as one of girls' motivation towards attempts to change the nature of school science. One of the main gains from the GIST project has been the clarification of what is meant by a 'girl friendly' science, that is a science which will appeal equally to the interests and concerns of girls as well as boys.

J. Whyte, in J. Whyte *et al.*, *Girl Friendly Schooling*, pp. 77, 78, 79.

Questions

1. The impact of gender on educational achievement is said to be a 'pedagogical issue'. What does this mean?
2. Why do you think
   (a) women working in science and technology were invited into schools?
   (b) single sex classes and groups were set up?
3. Give some examples of 'girl friendly' changes in science and technology curricula in your school or college.
4. To what extent are girls and women disadvantaged, outside education, by being scientifically and technically 'illiterate'?
5. If more girls do science and technology is this likely to change the nature of science and technology? If so, in what ways? If not, why not?

☐ Whose Knowledge?

Education is not benign or neutral but embodies a particular way of seeing the world. This, though, is a limited and distorted framework. Women's contributions, understandings and experiences are not represented or recorded. In another passage of her book Spender maintains 'schools cannot teach what society does not know'.

Reading 4

That we know little or nothing about women's traditions is directly related to the male control of education, for the problems of education are the problems that are decreed by men, and women's exclusion and disadvantage has not figured as a problem for men. While generation after generation of women has protested – often vehemently and to a wide audience – their words have 'disappeared' and this process continues to the present day. The process helps to maintain and perpetuate male control, and it is necessary to understand it, and the way it works, if we are to understand sexism and education. . . .

The problem is that the problems of men are only *half* the human problems. They constitute a one-sided view of the world and this encourages the construction of limited and distorted explanations (including the explanation that women are not among the 'greats' of our culture – which in turn 'proves' that women are inferior). . . .

From the position of subordination women can see that men miss much of the evidence and can construct only poorly informed explanations: women know a great deal about the world that men do not, they know a great deal about men that men do not know about themselves, and until women's view of the world coexists with men's view of the world, our entire system of education will be limited, distorted, sexist. Women have a responsibility to describe the world from the position they occupy – for other women: and for men, who will not know unless they are informed. If we wish to describe and analyse *human* experience, and to formulate explanations of the world which take *human beings* into account, then we must include the experience and understandings of women, as well as men. . . .

While males control education there is no direct means for women to pass on their understandings. What women know frequently dies with them, until feminists periodically rediscover them and their writing and attempt to reconstruct women's heritage and tradition. Each generation of women forges understandings about subordination, within their own lifetime and from the circumstances of their own lives, but because these meanings do not become the general currency of the culture they are not passed on to the next generation with the result that neither women nor men know about the women who have gone before.

So when men argue that male dominance is not a problem, that women have nothing to protest about, that there is no sexism in education, they are simply asserting – and quite rightly – that from their point of view it is *not* a problem. If women's point of view were equally valued – which it is not – we could just agree to differ, and attribute our different explanations to different experience. But women are subordinates – our view does not count as much as men's. It is men who have a problem, for they see little and assume they see all, they assume their experience is human experience – but human beings are not merely male.

D. Spender, *Invisible Women: The Schooling Scandal*, pp. 15–18.

Questions

1. What, according to the author, do we need to understand in order to explain sexism in education? Do you agree?
2. Consider the 'usual' contents of the following subjects and construct alternative/extra dimensions that might be included if both male and female experience were taken into account:
   (a) history
   (b) geography
   (c) art.
3. 'Women know a great deal about the world that men do not.' What do you understand by this statement? Explain and discuss it.

☐ Learning to be Female

Sara Delamont researched PE in schools as well as other lessons. Here she provides an extract from her fieldnotes. If the comments seem familiar to you it is because they are fairly commonplace and regarded (at least by teachers) as 'common sense'. It is important to remember that the ideals of femininity and gender-appropriate behaviour vary by class, region and race and there may be more than one stereotype within a large socially mixed and multi-ethnic school.

Reading 5

I go to girls' PE. They are all gathered into girls' changing room with two teachers who discuss what kit they should have. *Leotard*. If they have already got one, of any colour, that is OK. School also sells them. Leotard is needed for dance and gymnastics. A short skirt to be bought. Worn over leotard for netball and hockey . . . If you don't wear a leotard you must buy decent knickers for hockey because there are boys on the top field . . .

Goes over the rules for taking showers and swimming. The teachers keep a record of who has a shower/goes swimming. If they are 'on period' they must tell her (about showers and she'll put 'P' in book) and they are to tell the swimming master – he won't be embarrassed as he is a married man. Just say 'I'm on period'.

Discussing jewellery. Says it must all come off for PE except sleepers. One girl says her ring won't come off. Told tight rings are dangerous . . . told that especially dangerous when you get swelling in pregnancy. If they have a ring that is too tight they should get it cut off. (Try to get it off with soap first.) For PE must cover it with plaster.

(Later) Asks what can go into socks to protect legs in hockey.

'Shin pads.'

'Foam rubber.'

'Miss, newspaper.'

'Yes, borrow your dad's page three from *The Mirror*.'

Later, when inspecting the kit the girls actually have, finds one girl with a homemade skirt. Says 'If your mum's quite handy at needlework there's no reason why you shouldn't make your own.' PE staff say they prefer a skirt to shorts because girls get 'fatter' as they get older and because a skirt will 'cover your Dr White's'.

If they buy a skirt with an adjustable waist which wraps round it will last throughout their school life, and when they leave school, if they work in an office and want to play in the badminton team the skirt would do for that.

This long extract shows several examples of gender roles used to control the pupils. They have to wear certain clothes because of the boys. They should not wear tight jewellery because it will be dangerous when they are pregnant. Mother does the sewing, while father looks at nudes in the paper. Menstruation is normal and natural, but you must wear a skirt to avoid revealing the sanitary towel, you can't go swimming, and you must tell the swimming master who will check up on you but will not be embarrassed because he is married. And when you leave school, you are going to a job in an office. The underlying message of all this as regards gender roles is clear, and quite separate for each gender. The whole tone of the lesson was warm and friendly, and the teachers were bending over backwards to imply that poverty was not a stigma and expensive clothes were not necessary. Yet, they managed to miss several 'liberating' possibilities (tampons, playing badminton at university) and to imply that girls are headed for pregnancy after an office job. It would have been nice to see the same lesson for the boys.

S. Delamont, *Sex Roles and the School*, pp. 52–4.

Questions

1. What assumptions about gender roles does the author pick up from the teacher's comments?
2. In what ways are the girls expected to take account of boys?
3. What assumptions about the girls' futures are embodied in the teacher's remarks?

☐ Classroom Processes

Michelle Stanworth studied 'A' level classes in a college of further education. Here she focuses her attention on gender relations between teachers and pupils as an aspect of the fact that schooling is a different experience for males and females. If girls show stereotypical 'feminine' attributes these may run counter to the qualities expected of a 'good pupil' and vice versa.

Reading 6

Greater emphasis deserves to be placed, however, on those attitudes and actions of teachers which keep girls on the periphery of classroom activity. Teachers are (on their own accounts, and those of their pupils) concerned for boys, and attached to boys, more often than girls. They identify boys more readily than girls, and are reported to direct more questions and comments to their male pupils. Teachers of both sexes appear to permit the girls – even when they form the majority in the class – to be upstaged by the boys. In short, instead of drawing girls out, teachers in this study tend to go along with, and to reinforce the dominance of boys. A vicious circle is established: the less frequently girls are addressed, and encouraged to engage in classroom activity, the more that traditional beliefs about gender will appear to be vindicated – and the more girls are likely to be regarded as having nothing of value to communicate in the first place.

Male teachers have, on the evidence offered here, a heightened responsibility with regard to sexual divisions in the classroom. On their own accounts, men tend to differentiate more sharply between girls and boys in their attitudes and expectations than do women. Furthermore, pupils report that certain male teachers are noticeably more warm and sympathetic in their dealings with boys. In discussing what they experience as the favouritism of some male teachers towards boys, pupils often ventured to comment that male teachers experienced embarrassment or uneasiness in their relationships with girls. It is indeed possible that the age structure of teaching situations (older men dealing with younger girls, older women with younger boys) intersects with expectations about sexuality in such a way that it encourages male teachers to keep their distance from girls, in other words, if teachers wish to protect themselves from the appearance of sexual involvement with their pupils, then at present the male teacher-female pupil relationship is the one which is most likely to arouse suspicion. This may partially explain why female teachers seem to find less difficulty in expressing warmth towards pupils of the other sex than do men. But whatever the reasons for their attitudes and actions, male teachers must be encouraged to recognise (and to rectify) the damaging effects which their apparent leaning towards boys has on the class as a whole.

Discussion of the particular case of male teachers should not, however, be allowed to obscure a more central problem: why is it that teachers of both sexes are more likely to 'reject' girls, while showing a greater readiness to express attachment and concern for boys? Teachers involved in this study were, on the whole, conscientious and strongly committed to the welfare of their pupils. Some of the apparent insensitivity towards girls is, it seems to me, an *unintended* consequence of the guidelines teachers adopt when deciding how they will distribute, amongst their many pupils, their limited time and attention. Three major criteria for distinguishing 'deserving' pupils were mentioned by teachers in this study. Teachers felt that pupils who are trying hard, those who display outstanding ability, or pupils who are obviously experiencing difficulties with their work, should have first claim on their energies. On the surface, these criteria of commitment, talent and need may seem to be reasonable; but all three intersect with the initial reticence of girls in class so as to favour the choice of boys, rather than girls, as objects of the teacher's attention and concern.

M. Stanworth, *Gender and Schooling*, pp. 154–5.

Questions

1. What explanation does the author give for the attitudes of male teachers towards female pupils?
2. What three major criteria did these teachers adopt to determine 'deserving' pupils?
3. Why do these criteria result in more boys than girls being defined as 'deserving'?
4. What methods might a sociologist adopt to discover the 'amount of attention' devoted to particular pupils in a class?

□ Girls' Strategies

To be black, female and working class involves girls in more than one form of disadvantage; but such girls, in Mary Fuller's study, rejected the double stereotype of blackness and femininity and 'used' school for what it could offer them in terms of fulfilling their own goals. This study shows how schooling is mediated by girls themselves – they are not puppets. It also draws attention to their culture, showing them as active participants in their own schooling.

Reading 7

The subculture emerged from the girls' positive acceptance of the fact of being both black and female. Its particular flavour stemmed from their critical rejection of the meanings with which those categorizations are commonly endowed. Their consequent anger and frustration, unlike that of their black male peers, was not turned against themselves or translated into an automatic general dislike of whites or of the opposite sex. Rather their feelings and understandings gave particular meanings to achievement through the acquisition of educational qualifications.

The girls were all strongly committed to achievement through the job market, being marked out from the other girls not so much by the type of jobs to which they were aspiring as by the firmness with which they held their future job ambitions, and by their certainty that they would want to be employed whatever their future domestic circumstances might be. . . .

They were also strong believers in the value of education and educational qualifications as a necessary preparation for the 'good' jobs which they hoped to obtain – or more accurately, perhaps, they took such a belief for granted. They were confident of their ability to achieve the academic qualifications which they were aiming for, both in the short term (i.e. 'O' level and/or CSE) and in the longer term ('A' level and/or a variety of examinations to be taken at college, polytechnic or university).

This optimism extended to their wider life-chances. Conscious of actual incidents of racial discrimination and the possibility of discrimination against them because of their colour and sex, and aware of the high levels of unemployment locally and nationally which had double implications for them as young people and blacks, the girls nevertheless believed that in the job market there was much that they could do to forestall ending up in low level, dead-end jobs, or finding themselves unemployed on leaving school. They spoke of this in terms of being 'ambitious', but equally, ensuring that whatever ambitions they had were not deflected.

As will be clear, acquisition of academic qualifications was an integral part of this sense of control over their future. . . .

So far the picture drawn seems to be that of the girls as archetypal 'good' pupils – ones who have high aspirations and achieve well in public examinations – but this was far from the truth in most other aspects of their lives in school. Unlike other pupils who were similarly pro-education, the black girls were not pro-school. That is to say, their intolerance of the daily routines and their criticisms of much that went on inside the school were marked. They shared with some other pupils a view of school as 'boring', 'trivial' and 'childish', and yet at the same time were markedly different from these same pupils in that they had high aspirations and a high degree of academic success. Despite their critical view of school the black girls did not define it as 'irrelevant' (as did other pupils who found school boring, etc.), because of the particular importance which they attached to academic achievement. . . .

The black girls conformed to the stereotypes of the good pupil only in so far as they worked conscientiously at the schoolwork or homework set. But they gave all the appearances in class of not doing so, and in many other ways displayed an insouciance for the other aspects of the good pupil role. They neither courted a good reputation among teachers nor seemed to want to be seen as 'serious' by the staff or other pupils.

M. Fuller, in R. Deem (ed.), *Schooling for Women's Work*, pp. 57, 58, 59.

Questions

1. What are the elements of the girls' subculture as detailed here?
2. In what ways do these subcultural features relate to the non-school aspects of their lives?
3. If the girls had high aspirations and were pro-education, why were they not regarded as 'good pupils'?
4. In what ways are the girls rejecting stereotypes of blackness and femininity?

☐ Vocational Education and Training

The vocational education and youth training that most girls 'choose' follows traditional patterns. It is argued here that the ideologies of domesticity and femininity shape girls' education and training but in different ways for different classes. This is related to the way the labour market operates and utilises those ideologies. You should note the connections that are being suggested between historical, educational, cultural and employment processes.

Reading 8

Working-class education for both girls and boys has, historically, been vocational education; but for the girls the vocationalisation was imbued with a domestic ideology which attempted to teach them to be good wives and mothers if they were middle class, and to fit them for domestic occupations and be 'good women' if they were working class. The domestic ideology, in this sense, served both their home and labour market positions, although not without tensions. The ideology also served that stage of capital accumulation character-ised by the separation of home and work; by male occupations which required a great deal of domestic servicing; and by a cheap pool of local labour. It is crucial in attempting to understand current developments in education and training not only to consider the social positions for which different classes and genders are destined but also to remember that class divisions exist *within* gendered groups. This is a truism when applied to men; but the 'myth of female classlessness' both gives primacy to a domestic ideology which homogenises women and also does not facilitate consideration of the very different nature of working-class girls' education and train-ing.

For younger women, clerical and shop jobs currently account for 43 per cent of their occupations nationally. The fact that just over one-third of YTS places offered are on clerical and service sector courses is therefore congruent with the actual labour market. Girls are encouraged to enter these areas of the labour market by the fact that the occupations are often presented with a 'glamorous' image; the distinction between office and factory work is the crux of the difference between a 'good' job and a 'bad' one for girls. Not only are the conditions of office working thought to be better; but it is also a site where an idealised form of femininity is represented and it is also a setting where girls think they might meet the 'right sort of man', and that it holds the illusion of upward mobility.

Office work can, of course, accommodate a wide range of girls and the skill of typing is only part of the requirement for the job. One survey of male managers found they looked for 'personality, good grooming, clear speech and a sense of humour'. . . . however, it is difficult in our society to disentangle notions of personality from those of gender; and where employers have an 'embarrassment of choice' with regard to workers the situation may facilitate the operation of personal preference and social stereotypes more than under conditions of low demand for jobs. Shop work can also be seen as an appropriate work setting if the shop concerned sells fashion goods or expensive items, where dealing with the commodities at a service level has higher status than manufacturing them. The public presentation of the secretarial image and 'boutique' assistant through the media and advertising is one that defines the elements of work in close connection with expectations about stereotyped female behaviour and appearance. These expectations will be not only a powerful determinant over which particular girls obtain such jobs as exist but also influential over the girls themselves.

C. Buswell, in C. Glendinning and J. Millar (eds), *Women and Poverty*, pp. 74, 75, 76.

Questions

1. What was the importance, historically, of the domestic ideology in terms of the education of both middle-class and working-class girls?
2. 'The myth of "female classlessness" gives primacy to a domestic ideology that homogenises women.' What do you understand by this statement?
3. What are the features of shop and office jobs that appeal to many girls? Why?
4. How might the ideology of femininity affect employers and employment?

Essay Questions

1. Examine the contention that the educational system reproduces gender relationships. (Cambridge 1984)
2. What contribution have feminists made to our understanding of educational processes and outcomes?
3. What differences, if any, are there between the educational experiences of boys and girls? Do any differences influence the comparative levels of achievement of boys and girls? (Oxford 1984)

Further Reading

S. Acker, 'Sociology, gender and education', in S. Acker *et al.*, *Women and Education*. A consideration of the ways different sociological approaches explain the position of women and the application of these approaches to educational questions.

R. Deem, *Schooling for Women's Work*. This is a collection of articles, many based on original research, that together cover many of the aspects of education that are mentioned in this chapter.

R. Deem, *Coeducation Reconsidered*. Chapters by different authors on the history, politics and realities of coeducation which raise important sociological questions with regard to girls' schooling.

S. Delamont, *Sex Roles and the School*. A fascinating book that discusses a wide range of literature and research sociologically: it is also interesting and easy to follow.

G. Frith, 'Little women, good wives: is English good for girls?' in A. McRobbie and T. McCabe (eds), *Feminism for Girls*. As a contrast to the discussion on science, this chapter looks at how English has come to be 'gendered' female and why girls do it.

R. Meyenn, 'School girls peer groups', in P. Woods (ed.), *Pupil Strategies*. A study of girls showing that school control over appearance and dress was the critical determinant of girls' responses to school.

D. Spender and E. Sarah (eds), *Learning to Lose*. There is an important section in this book on women teachers, with chapters by Clarricoates, Buchan and Whitbread.

D. Spender, *Invisible Women: The Schooling Scandal*. A very readable, radical, account of the way in which women and girls are subjected to male-dominated education which is presented as objective knowledge.

M. Stanworth, *Gender and Schooling*. A study of 'A' level students in a college of further education showing the processes of education that operate to exclude girls from much classroom interaction.

J. Whyte *et al.*, *Girl Friendly Schooling*. Contributions by different authors, from different backgrounds, on what makes schooling unfriendly to girls and examples of interventions that have been tried.

5 | Women and employment

☐ Introduction

The presence of women in paid employment outside the home is not a new phenomenon, but the postwar period has seen an increasing number of married women in the labour market. In spite of the Equal Pay Act, which came into force in 1975, women do not on average earn the same as men; this is partly accounted for by the fact that they do not, by and large, do the same jobs but are concentrated in particular areas of the *labour market*. There is in fact more than one 'market' for labour, so it has been described as a dual labour market; but, as the extract from Garnsey *et al.* points out, this is a simplification: 'segmented labour market' is the term now most often used.

The way in which jobs are organised and the content of the tasks performed is called the *labour process*. The greatest changes currently taking place with regard to this process are to do with the increasing use of technology, especially micro-electronics, which is not only changing the amount of paid work but also the content of the employment that remains.

Women's relationship to paid work is, however, seen differently from that of men to their jobs, sometimes leading people to assume that the circumstances described in the following extracts are not of serious consequence. It is assumed that for men, paid employment provides the basis for all other activities and for their self-identity and sense of worth; but for women it is assumed that the family is the basis for their other activities and they are often thought neither to be so attached to their job nor to suffer as greatly if it disappears. Many women, however, are not in households where they are supported by another wage, and even if they are the other wage is often inadequate to provide the sole family support. Whether or not their wage is the only one, earning it has provided women with some financial independence within the family and its loss returns them to the position of having to 'ask' for everything.

Women have been described as a 'reserve army of labour', drawn into employment when the economy is expanding and expelled back into the home during recessions. Women make good candidates for this role as they can be made to 'disappear' from the public arena. More recently, though, some writers such as Walby (1986) have maintained that the historical and empirical evidence does not totally support this view, as women did not leave the labour force during the recessions of the 1930s, or more recently in the 1970s, as illustrated by the extract from Pahl. The issue is complicated by the fact that the areas of employment in which women predominate, particularly in the service sector, have been growing, and this may have cushioned them to some extent from the tendency to shed labour in recent decades. For this reason, the 'reserve army' debate is still being conducted as labour market changes are still occurring. Another complicating factor is that many married women have nothing to gain, in terms of benefits, by registering as unemployed so the full extent of female unemployment – that is, the number of women who would wish to work if jobs were available – is simply not known. It was estimated in 1981 (Mori Poll) that it was a million higher than in official statistics.

The growth of employment in the service sector has helped women resist unemployment. Nonetheless, women have remained in the labour market on a different basis. In the United Kingdom almost one half of all employed women work part-time; this is one of the highest proportions of part-time women employees in all EEC countries. Part-time employment in this country is badly paid, contains few prospects and usually means that protective employment legislation does not apply to the workers; many state benefits that derive from full national insurance payments are also not available. The assumption that paid work is an 'extra' activity for women strongly influences both government policies that determine benefit entitlement and employers' policies regarding how they organise their workforce. It is commonly held that part-time jobs exist because that is the only basis on which women will work, but the extract by Robinson maintains that it is more for the benefit of employers; although, as Sharpe points out in the last extract, women are constrained in the ways in which they themselves can participate in the labour market.

All these factors indicate a bleak picture, but you should consider to what extent the labour market could operate differently for both men and women and to what extent changes could be generated by different government policies, employers' practices and the nature of men's and women's other responsibilities.

☐ 1945 and Beyond

The way in which women's employment is viewed has changed depending on the extent to which their labour has been needed outside the home. Pahl also talks of the 'ideological bias' in social policies, which contained certain assumptions about women's role – but women themselves had other ideas.

Reading 1

The employment of married women remained very stable at around 10 per cent of all married women until the start of the Second World War. By 1945 the number of married women employed was over 2.5 million, that is, more than five times the number in paid work before the war. This is probably a substantial underestimate of the number of married women workers, many of whom would have engaged in essential work on a voluntary basis. For example, there were 2,000 British Restaurants: some of these were run by voluntary committees and some married women worked in them without pay, although these were a minority. As we have seen, many married women in employment before the war were (certainly in south-east England) 'deviants' – shaming their husbands, who felt that this demonstrated that they were not looking after them properly. However, during the war public opinion changed radically. As Gertrude Williams remarked at the time: 'War necessity has swung public opinion so far the other way that the woman who does *not* add to her household duties feels guilty and apologetic, and there is no doubt that if, after the war, society looked upon it as normal to combine home and work the majority of women should do what was expected of them.

If women were to follow all Williams' prescriptions they would stay at home with their children (which it was their natural duty to have) until they had 'launched' them – at whatever mature age that would be. Then they would look for jobs that could be undertaken 'with only the scantiest previous experience'. Restaurants and personal service were two of the areas that Williams thought were likely to provide suitable employment for women, whose lives were set to a different pattern from those of men.

These assumptions were firmly built into the post-war period of reconstruction managed by the Labour Party. Perhaps the clearest embodiment of these principles can be seen in the way New Towns were planned. Neighbourhood units were laid out some distance from the main shopping and recreational facilities in the town centre, with just a few shops within walking distance for daily needs. Men went to the industrial estates, segregated some distance from the main living areas, so that earning and consuming were kept physically separated. There was no expectation that women would want to have employment near to their homes or that opportunities for part-time work might encourage women to combine the care of small children with paid employment.

There was no absolute reduction in the number of married women working in the period immediately following the Second World War, but the female labour force as a whole did decline in the late 1940s as single women married and started their families. By the early 1950s, the proportion of married women in employment (one in four) returned to the level it had been in 1851: the rigours of married women's domestic imprisonment seemed to be abating. Despite the ideological bias in the social policies and programmes of the immediate post-war period, married women in employment began to increase both proportionately and absolutely. Numbers employed rose from 2.85 million in 1950 to 3.77 million in 1957, the latter figure being about half of the total of all female workers. Inevitably, however, conventional attitudes were maintained, even by Viola Klein, the author of a sociological survey of *Britain's Married Women Workers* published in 1965:

> It is not suggested here that it is – or is likely to become so in the near future – the general practice for married women to accept employment away from their homes. Housewives without jobs, after all, still outnumber those in employment by 2 to 1; and as something like half of them have one or more children under the age of 16, the size of the reserve that can be drawn on will probably always remain limited to a minority of married women.

Despite recognizing that the trends towards the greater employment of married women would continue, Klein completely misread the situation: the middle 1960s were the beginning of an unprecedented increase in the proportion of married women in employment. By the early 1980s there were about 10.5 million women in the labour force, representing two-thirds of all women between 16 and 60.

R.E. Pahl, *Divisions of Labour*, pp. 78–9.

Questions

1. Describe and account for the changing female employment rate since 1945 as outlined in this passage.
2. What were the 'assumptions' that were built into post-war policies? Were they present in other policies besides those of town planning?
3. What factors do you think led women to prove Viola Klein's prediction wrong?

☐ The Terms of Women's Employment

The first diagram by Dex illustrates 'event histories' for women of different ages and combines events at home and in employment. When you have considered this diagram you should look at the table of average earnings for men and women in 1984, remembering that the Equal Pay Act came into operation in 1975.

Reading 2

Illustration of a selection of plotted event histories for women of different ages

Key

Event history starts when women leave school and ends at the interview

1 Stopped work
2 Starts full-time work
3 Starts part-time work
6 Marriage

8 Childbirth
9 Death of child
12 Interview

Underlining

━━━ full-time
working period

---- part-time
working period

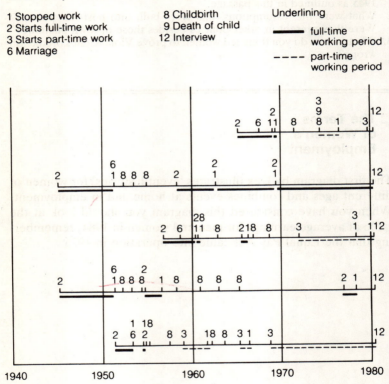

S. Dex, *Women's Work Histories: An Analysis of the Women and Employment Survey*, Research Paper no. 46. Department of Employment, 1984, p. 9.

Gross weekly earnings of full-time employees[1]: by sex (Great Britain, £s and percentages)

	Males					Females				
	1970	1981	1983	1985	1986	1970	1981	1983	1985	1986
Manual employees										
Mean (£s)	26.4	120.2	141.6	163.6	174.4	13.4	74.7	88.1	101.3	107.5
Median (£s)	25.3	112.8	133.1	153.3	163.4	12.8	71.6	84.3	95.3	101.1
As percentage of median										
Highest decile	148	151	152	155	155	145	143	145	150	150
Lowest decile	66	69	67	66	65	70	70	69	69	69
Non-manual employees										
Mean (£s)	35.2	160.5	191.8	225.0	244.9	18.0	97.5	116.1	133.8	145.7
Median (£s)	31.0	147.0	173.9	202.4	219.4	16.0	87.7	105.6	122.0	131.5
As percentage of median										
Highest decile	176	167	171	172	175	174	172	164	163	167
Lowest decile	60	60	59	58	57	64	68	66	66	65
All employees										
Mean (£s)	29.5	138.2	164.7	192.4	207.5	16.4	92.0	109.5	126.4	137.2
Median (£s)	26.8	124.6	148.1	172.8	185.1	14.7	82.8	99.5	115.2	123.4
As a percentage of median										
Highest decile	162	168	170	171	173	169	172	167	164	170
Lowest decile	64	64	63	61	60	67	68	66	66	65

[1]Figures relate to April each year and to full-time employees on adult rates whose pay for the survey pay-period was not affected by absence.
Source: New Earnings Survey, Department of Employment: from *Social Trends*, HMSO 1988, p. 85.

Questions

1. Using the first diagram describe the typical '*employment histories*' of women of different ages.
2. Is the employment history of a woman starting paid work in the mid-1980s likely to differ from that of a woman who started employment in the 1940s and one who started in the 1960s? If so, in what ways and why?
3. Using the table list the jobs in which women predominate that might be included in the 'female manual' and the 'female non-manual' categories.
4. Is there 'equal pay'? Give reasons for your answer.

□ The Segmented Labour Market

One of the reasons why women do not earn the same as men is because they are concentrated in different jobs, as the labour market is *segmented*. This means there is more than one labour market and each one tends to be inhabited by different kinds of people. Jobs, in other words, tend to be done by either women or men, the young or middle-aged, black or white. You may need to read this passage several times as it is attempting to describe a complex process in relatively few words.

Reading 3

Before we examine sources of supply of labour and the interaction of supply and demand we need to examine the differentiation of demand for labour. Differences stem from variations in the constraints under which firms operate, the alternatives open to employers and the employment strategies they pursue. Complex patterns emerge within this diversity, but it is possible to classify categories of employment in the simplest terms according to whether they provide good pay, security and prospects (termed *primary employment conditions*) or fail to do so (termed *secondary employment conditions*). Diverse occupations are found within both sectors; they cannot readily be defined in terms of job content or qualifications. The starting point for the analysis of labour market segmentation is the shortage of good jobs; this rather than the shortage of 'good quality labour' is the crucial factor.

It should be noted that the use of the term 'primary' and 'secondary' to describe employment conditions is quite different from that used to describe the nature of an industry. Primary industries are raw-materials producing industries (such as agriculture and mining) while secondary industries are manufacturing industries.

The use of 'primary' and 'secondary' to describe employment conditions suggests the existence of a dual labour market (i.e., two separate labour markets) but this is a simplification. The market for labour is neither unitary nor dual. Structured patterns of demand interact with diverse sources of supply to create what can be thought of as a set of segmented markets for labour, relatively isolated from each other. In the literature on segmented labour markets variations abound on the themes of primary and secondary employment.

Primary and secondary employment conditions are essentially ideal types rather than descriptions of facts. We further need to distinguish between industries, firms (or employing organizations) and occupations; all three categories provide both relatively secure and well paid (primary type) and also insecure and badly paid (secondary type) employment. In the simplest terms *industries* which provide primary employment conditions are those consisting of a majority of *firms* (or employing organizations) providing primary employment conditions; usually these industries consist of large firms using modern technology, facing predictable demand for their products and exerting some control over their product markets. Industries providing primary sector employment are generally characterized by strong collective bargaining organizations. Industries providing secondary employment can be defined simply in terms of the absence of provision of primary conditions of employment. Within each set of industries are groups of sub-markets with boundaries which shift over time.

The most obvious evidence of the *industrial* basis for labour market segmentation (LMS) is provided by differences in pay and employment conditions for the same occupation in different industries. For occupations which are similar across industries there are systematic differences in pay and conditions; for example, haulage drivers in industries providing primary employment conditions are paid at higher rates than in industries providing secondary employment conditions. . . .

Nevertheless, the production conditions of industries do not fully explain the provision of secure and stable jobs. Political and cultural factors affecting industries are also at work, as is shown by examining employment conditions in the same industry in different countries. There are differences in the provision of primary employment conditions in a given industry in different industrialized countries, despite similar technological and product market conditions. . . .

Within firms providing good employment conditions, secondary type jobs are frequently found. There are two general patterns, primary employment conditions may be reserved for an elite, e.g., of managerial or professional staff. Alternatively a minority of workers may have secondary employment conditions in contrast with the bulk of the employees. The retail (shopping) industry provides an example of firms where a mainly male managerial hierarchy has employment conditions which contrast with those of the mass of mainly female sales workers. In many firms where most employees enjoy primary status, secondary employment conditions apply to part-time, temporary or seasonal workers, who are not treated as internal employees. But these conditions may also apply to a stable and regular category of jobs within the firm, as in the case of cleaners or canteen workers. The coexistence of primary and secondary jobs affords managers both work-force stability and the ability to off-load the costs of flexibility on to more vulnerable sections of the work-force.

E. Garnsey, J. Rubery and F. Wilkinson, in R. Deem and G. Salaman (eds), *Work, Culture and Society*, pp. 52–4.

Questions

1. What is meant by 'labour market segmentation'?
2. Define the characteristics of both primary and secondary employment conditions. Give *three* examples of each.
3. Why are women more likely to be in jobs characterised by secondary employment conditions?

☐ Changes in the Labour Process

The nature of employment and the way it is organised are changing rapidly with the introduction of technology, particularly micro-electronics. Office work is an area of employment for a large number of women, and changes here will affect them considerably if they remain in employment; but micro-electronic equipment also contains the potential to make many workers redundant.

Reading 4

Today, throughout the industrialized countries, one of the fundamental characteristics of the labour markets is the marked segregation by sex. Women are concentrated in a limited range of occupations and are most likely to be found working in relatively less skilled and lower-paying jobs than their male counterparts. This concentration has important implications, because many of the occupations to which women gravitate are those that the new information technology is beginning to transform.

Microelectronic technology has the capability of profoundly affecting so-called information activities – the creation, processing, storage, and transmission of information. A large proportion of the workforce in most countries is engaged in these activities. In the US, it has been estimated that about half of the labour force work in information-related occupations; in the UK the information sector is said to employ nearly half of all workers.

The information sector, like the rest of the economy, is not homogeneous. Within it there are skilled occupations – those that create, analyze, coordinate, and interpret information – and less skilled – those that manipulate information. The latter's tasks may be characterized as information-handling. It is in these activities that women by and large are concentrated as secretaries, typists, bookkeepers, stenographers, cashiers, and the like. In contrast, the upper echelons of information occupations are dominated by men, who comprise the vast majority of senior and middle management and professional workers. Microelectronics is conceived of fundamentally as a tool to assist the latter group in their decision-making, analysis, and communication by speeding up and broadening the flow of information to and from them. The use of microelectronics, as far as the information-handlers are concerned, is a tool to increase their productivity in delivery of that information and consequently has more significant employment implications.

Looking at the information-handling occupations, the degree of sex segregation becomes evident. If, following the analysis of Joy Selby Smith, a 'female' occupation can be defined as one in which 50 per cent or more workers engaged in that occupation are women, one finds women workers overwhelmingly concentrated in a few 'female' occupations. Many of these are information-handling occupations. Selby Smith found that in Australia over 85 per cent of women in the paid workforce were concentrated in 18 of 61 occupations listed by the Statistical Office, all of them 'female' occupations.

Half of Australian women were found to be in 'female' occupations that were likely to feel a significant impact from developments in microelectronics.

Using detailed labour force data, a similar analysis can be performed for the US. About one-third of all women workers are concentrated in white-collar female occupations – mainly clerical – which are expected to be affected by the use of microelectronic technology. Only 16 per cent are classified as professional and technical workers. When one looks at management occupations, the proportion is smaller again – only 6 per cent. Those information-handling occupations – bookkeepers, secretaries, cashiers, typists and so on – are clearly dominated by women: in many of these occupations more than 90 per cent of these workers are women.

In the UK one-third of women work in offices and of these more than 90 per cent are employed in routine clerical jobs. The top three female occupations are clerical, cashiers, and typists. It is likely that similar concentrations are found elsewhere in the industrialized countries.

This analysis of occupational data does not mean that one-half of all Australian women or one-third of women in the US are being threatened by job loss as the result of the use of microelectronics in the office. But it does suggest that large numbers of women bear the burden of the adjustments that are required. Moreover, it is not just those women who are now employed that will be affected. It may cause problems among women who are seeking to re-enter the workforce after a spell in domestic activity and among new entrants hoping to follow in the tradition of the women before them.

D. Werneke, in T. Forrester (ed.), *The Information Technology Revolution*, pp. 400–2.

Questions

1. Give examples of jobs in the 'information sector' in the United Kingdom.
2. What are the 'burdens of adjustment' that women will be expected to bear?
3. Office automation has not, in all instances, proceeded as rapidly as the available technology would make possible. Can you think of any factors relating to the nature of office employment that might account for this?

□ The Nature of Work

Many women work in 'service occupations' and changes in the nature of their jobs are seen by us, the customers or clients, in a particular way. This extract illustrates the effect that changes in the nature of work might have on the employee herself. Next time you go to a supermarket, you might bear this in mind and see if you can spot a 'worn out' checkout worker!

Reading 5

Being a till operator

Working as a till operator is a tiring job; people think you are just sitting there not doing anything, but you are. You are moving stock: in the years I have been there, I must have moved the whole of the stock of the Superstore through. As the customer goes through the checkout the till operator has to pick up each item with their left hand and put it in the trolley – a big bag of potatoes can be very heavy. People think 'That's a nice job, you are just sitting there', but really you get very tired because you are using a lot of muscles: you put pressure on your back, in your feet, you really are working every part of your body. I only worked part-time, but even my shoulder, the one you use to lift all the things into the trolley, sometimes ached; I should imagine anyone who had done it all day long must really ache across the back.

As far as other people are concerned, it is just a job with no skill attached to it, a job that takes no effort, but what they forget is the stress factor. All the time you are sitting on that till you have to concentrate, customers are coming through all the time and you cannot drop your concentration for a minute. It was very different in the past. When I first started working 40 years ago, the hours were much longer – the normal working week for shop assistants was something like 48 hours – but the pace was so much slower. Now, for nearly all the three, or sometimes four hours, I was on the till, I was going at full pitch.

Years ago a customer would come in, you would sell them whatever they wanted, you would have a little chat and then perhaps you would get another customer. You did not have a whole queue waiting for you all the time; they came in for the whole process; jobs have now been cut up into little sections. It was so much nicer to go through the whole process; serving the customer and taking the money; it was so much more human. Nowadays you do not look after your own stock. Years ago when I worked at the Co-op, nothing was pre-packed; we had to weigh and pack everything like sugar, dried fruit, everything like that; so when there were no customers, there you were weighing all this stuff and packing it into bags ready for the customers when they came in. Customers were people then, now they come through the checkout like robots.

In those days you did not get anywhere near so tired. I know that I am older now, but even the youngsters at the Superstore get absolutely worn out. People often say the youngsters do not work, but they do, management expects every ounce they can get out of them. Things are just so much faster nowadays everyone has far more pressure put on them. I know they have cut the hours down, but not to that extent.

The management do not work out the kind of stress that is involved in the job as it is nowadays. If it was something very important, say someone's life was at stake, they would probably go into all the stress factors, but because the effects of this kind of stress are not so obvious, nobody is bothered.

J. Kuhn, in T. Scarlett Epstein, K. Crehan, A. Genzer and J. Sass (eds), *Women, Work and Family in Britain and Germany*, pp. 167–8.

Questions

1. What changes in the labour process (the nature of work and the way it is organised) associated with selling does this shop assistant describe?
2. What advantages for the firm do these changes bestow?
3. To what extent will changes in the labour process allow different kinds of employment policies by the firm?

□ Part-time Work

The employment history of many women contains a period of part-time work, as the earlier diagram by Dex illustrated (see Reading 2). Part-time employment is the only kind possible for some women with family responsibilities, but in this extract Robinson argues that it serves employers themselves better than the people they employ, and many women are working in these jobs because they are the only ones available.

Reading 6

The features which distinguish part-time from full-time jobs are familiar. Part-time employment is concentrated in the services sector of the economy, is largely female, and is relatively low paid. At June 1984 almost 90 per cent of total part-time employment of 4.9 million was in services. The trend towards higher levels of employment in service industries in Britain is evident from the 1920s and has been intensified by the decline in manufacturing reflected in the loss of 1.9 million jobs in manufacturing, 95 per cent of which were those of full-time employees, compared with the increase of 1.7 million in service industries, 70 per cent of which were part-time.

Female part-timers, the majority married women, account for 84 per cent of all part-time workers, and for 46 per cent of female employees. They work largely in service activities; the rise in their numbers from 2.8 million to 3.8 million between 1971 and 1981 occurred wholly within service industries, compared with a reduction of 85,000 in manufacturing. Approximately two thirds of the increase was in the private sector distributive trades, banking, insurance and finance, catering and leisure industries. The use of female part-time labour in manufacturing it should be noted is not insignificant despite the comparatively small numbers involved. In relative terms the part-time proportion of female employment in all manufacturing industries in 1981 was 23 per cent, which was higher than the 1971 level of 20 per cent. . . .

The way in which employers in a variety of industries make use of part-time workers is shown by their hours of work, occupations and pay. In food manufacturing establishments, where from 33 to 87 per cent of the female labour force in manual occupations work part-time, production is maintained over 15–16 hour days by employing full-time, day workers and separate shifts of a.m., p.m. and evening workers on production and packing jobs. The timing of work schedules eliminates loss of output due to mealbreaks, thus maximizing the use of capital equipment by adding approximately 1 to 2 hours to daily production time without incurring extra costs from premium rates of pay for overtime or the rotating shifts worked by full-timers. In tobacco manufacturing a factory operating a 4½-day week employs part-time alongside full-time labour to ensure continuity of production during the lunch break from Monday to Thursday. The afternoon shift works for 16½ hours over four days, giving an untypically short part-time working week for manufacturing industry; at other factories of the same company part-timers work on five days for 17½ to 25 hours per week. In engineering part-time hours are adjusted in response to fluctuations in product demand; during slack periods weekly hours can be shortened, minimizing the need for dismissals and enabling management to retain experienced labour and reduce the costs of recruitment and training when demand rises. Part-timers' hours have been altered to maintain output over an unchanged working day at plants where the length of the full-time working week was reduced from 40 to 37½ hours; 30 per cent of the part-time workers' weekly hours were reduced from 25 to 20, and those of another 5 per cent from 25 to 22½ hours. . . .

The patterns of employers' labour requirements are thus the main reason for the employment of part-time labour; part-time jobs exist in their own right and are not regarded as fractions of full-time jobs. Part-time workers are not engaged as substitutes for full-time employees in short supply. The only notable exception is nursing, where there are high rates of labour turnover amongst full-time qualified nurses. In organizations with significant levels of part-time employment managers have waiting lists of women seeking full-time jobs and of part-time employees wishing to transfer to full-time work. While there are employers who say that the increased size of the labour force generates additional recruitment, training and administration costs, they do not attempt to reduce them by substituting full-time for part-time labour. Furthermore, in companies which have undergone long-term reductions in overall levels of employment, the relative size of the female part-time labour force has not been adversely affected.

O. Robinson, in *National Westminster Bank Quarterly Review*, pp. 20–5.

Questions

1. Describe the 'transfer of labour resources' that has occurred since the 1970s.
2. What advantages for employers and disadvantages for employees does the shift towards part-time employment imply?
3. Why do women comprise the majority of part-time workers? What assumptions about women underpin these changes in the labour market?

□ The
Dual
Role

Part-time, temporary and undemanding employment for women is provided because it is assumed that paid work is not their central interest. Women themselves, however, do 'sell their labour power' under different circumstances from most men, and this is what Sharpe discusses.

Reading 7

Most employers have little knowledge of or concern about the family responsibilities of their female employees, and even less about their male employees. It is taken for granted that they have no obligation to make allowances for these aspects of workers' lives. Working women with children are expected to fit in with the timetables of industry and productivity. At the same time, all women, whether or not they have husbands or children, are none the less assumed to have current or future family commitments that will hinder their working potential. This has profound effects on women's opportunities and prospects as employers still hold a full hand of prejudices against women workers and tend to view them as an unstable workforce at any stage in their lives. It is thought that young single girls do not take work seriously enough, move between jobs and eventually leave work when they have children, if not before. Women with children are considered unreliable because of their childcare responsibilities which mean that they are sometimes unpunctual or have to take time off. Working mothers, especially part-timers, are stereotyped as temporary, unreliable, uncommitted employees who do not view their work as important and therefore neither warrant nor receive the wages, rights or respect given to male workers. When women apply for jobs they know they may be interviewed and assessed as much on the basis of their family situation as their ability to do the work. . . .

The search for a convenient job and a sympathetic boss, preference for part-time work and low participation in union activities, are some of the consequences for working mothers of the conditions under which they have to sell their labour, that is, predominantly to suit the family, not themselves. When they have children, most women – and working-class women in particular – leave their jobs with no imminent plans to return. It is women with more education and training (and hence usually middle-class women) who have greater access to more interesting and better paid jobs, and have more chance of continuing in one line of work. But as prospective working mothers, they all face the same problems of combining family responsibilities with a job, and at whatever moment they contemplate returning to work, they survey a familiar and barren occupational landscape. While the children are still dependent, jobs are valued more for their convenience and flexibility, and those most commonly taken by working mothers, such as cleaning, waitressing, canteen work, shelf-stacking, and so on, bear little resemblance to the jobs suggested in their career advice at school. Most girls leave school and seek jobs in an already limited range of 'women's work', but when they return to the workforce after a break to have their children, they move within an even narrower spectrum of jobs, circumscribed by their role in the family.

> I've got a very jaundiced attitude of getting a job when I leave college. I don't hold out much hope of being able to get a really good job with good hours, or an employer that will accept that I've also got children without really having to fight for my rights, because they're automatically going to expect me to stay off work if the children are ill, so I'm a bad employment risk. . . . I feel that if a place is willing to accept a woman with a child, then they've got to realize what all the consequences are. You can't just say, well, you can come here and we'll give you the job providing you deny the existence of your children. You can't do it.
>
> (Joanne, university student with 5-year-old daughter)

S. Sharpe, *Double Identity: The Lives of Working Mothers*, pp. 55–69.

Questions

1. What are the 'full hand of prejudices against women workers' that employers are said to hold? Explain why they do.
2. Discuss the conditions under which mothers have to 'sell their labour power'. What are the differences between different mothers and different occupations?
3. In what ways might childcare, housework and employment be organised differently, for both men and women, to alleviate the inequality in employment?

Essay Questions

1. 'Despite their increasing share of the labour market, women are not employed evenly throughout the occupational structure.' What explanations have sociologists offered for this situation?
   (AEB June 1986)
2. 'Part-time employment is both a barrier to women's equality at work and also the only means by which some of them can participate in employment at all.' Explain and discuss.
3. How would you explain the fact that most women's jobs are less skilled, more menial and less well-paid than those of men?
   (WJEC June 1984)
4. Discuss the impact of the increasing use of technology in service sector jobs on women's employment.

Further Reading

C. Bell, 'Work, non-work and unemployment – a discussion', in R. Burgess (ed.), *Exploring Society*. Whilst not specifically about gender this chapter locates paid work in the context of other work and the section on the labour market describes its segmentation in a very straightforward, albeit brief, manner.

A. Game and R. Pringle, *Gender at Work*. An Australian book which not only discusses the role of technology in the service sector but has interesting empirical data and descriptions of some service occupations.

M. Herzog, *From Hand to Mouth: Women and Piecework*. A grim account of women workers in modern West German factories, producing goods with household names. It deals with the nature of piecework, boredom and the fear of unemployment in addition to coping with other responsibilities.

A. Oakley, *Subject Women*. Section 3 is a straightforward account of the relationship of women to paid and unpaid work, both historically and in other cultures. It also mentions changes in the labour market, part-time earnings and service occupations.

A. Pollert, *Girls, Wives, Factory Lives*. A study of women in a tobacco factory. The different ways in which married and unmarried women perceive their work is well illustrated, as is the way that they are themselves seen by their union and employers. From their own speech the importance of other aspects of their lives is brought out.

T. Scarlett Epstein *et al.*, *Women, Work and Family in Britain and Germany*. An interesting book which contains case study material from some service occupations and discussion of the relationship between paid work and housework, Trade Unions and the relationship between male managers and female employees.

S. Sharpe, *Double Identity: the Lives of Working Mothers*. This book is constructed around interviews with employed mothers in different parts of the country. It is easy to read and demonstrates the various 'meanings' that paid work has for the women.

J. West (ed.), *Work, Women and the Labour Market*. Interesting case studies on women's employment in specific jobs including clerical work and the clothing industry. Also broader discussions of women's position in the labour market.

6 | Women and the media

Stereotypes of women as represented in the media are an important aspect of sociological theorising and research concerning the position of women in modern society. In looking at the presentation of gender in advertisements, television programmes, magazines and so on, it is possible to scrutinise them for the manufacturers' stereotypes concerning the differences between the sexes and also for what they tell us about prevalent gender patterns. Simply looking, however, at these aspects – important though they are – will not tell us what purposes the stereotypes serve nor why and to what extent they are successful in either maintaining or generating ideas about gender roles. Firstly it is necessary to consider the nature of stereotypes in general, and the first extract by Perkins clearly lists features of a stereotype and the groups to which they are usually applied. It is important to remember that stereotypes can only exist in a social, not a private sense, because they are based on shared meanings and understandings: they are not, though, simple reflections of social values but are *selections* of particular values and their perceived relevance to specific social roles. Stereotypes often develop about a group that has presented a 'problem', so most stereotypes concern oppressed groups because the dominant group's position is relatively stable and unproblematic. The second important thing to remember is that positive stereotypes are an important part of ideology and the stereotypes of major structural groups are supported by laws, traditions and institutions (see Chapter 2 in relation to social policies and women's role in the family). Although all the extracts in this chapter deal with representations of women you should also consider the representations of men to see how the images relate to one another.

Theories of media studies now reject the idea that people react passively to messages addressed to them: the way a person receives and appropriates the message is seen to be important. The media, nonetheless, have an important role in redefining stereotypes and circulating new definitions and meanings and certainly the modern media accept several different ways of conceiving women's role and image. The second extract, from a TUC booklet, illustrates newspaper accounts of two events involving women where their achievements have been reported in terms of traditional, and limited, definitions of women's roles and attributes. Although not all newspaper representations are as crude as these examples, nevertheless most women who are reported in the press are linked to their family background, marital status and appearance – thus bringing aspects of female stereotypes into play. You will notice, when looking at representations in the media, that there are actually relatively few stereotypes of men compared with the large number for women, but as about a quarter of most newspapers are deliberately oriented towards the (stereotyped?) interests of males perhaps this is not surprising.

Of all the media representations of women, advertisements have received most attention, not only because they are widespread and obvious but also because advertising itself is far from being simply a naive way to sell goods. Advertisements sell us not only commodities but also an image of ourselves if we buy or use the goods. As Williamson (1978, 12) explains, 'material things we need are made to represent other, non-material things we need – the point of exchange between the two is where 'meaning' is created'. This is where the number of female stereotypes becomes important, as 'images' can be sold in connection with women's domestic, childcare, employment and beautification roles, creating a multiplicity of possibilities for advertisers. The third extract by Mamay and Simpson describes the three main roles that television advertisements use and their findings about who does and says what in such advertisements. Besides the stereotypes portrayed in advertisements there is a further stage where women, having been 'produced' in a certain image, are used to sell less exciting products such as washing machines, life insurance and so on. There is thus a kind of circularity where women are 'sold back' to themselves.

Women's magazines are an interesting aspect of media representations of women as, like the girls' magazines discussed in Chapter 3, they are aimed at women themselves. The covers of such magazines, almost without exception, show a smiling, white woman's face, and it is this image, above all, that is presented as the 'normal' and 'natural' representation of the feminine woman in our society. The extract by Ferguson discusses the role of women's magazines in the cult of femininity and in offering women a positive evaluation of themselves within that cult. The question of the effectiveness of these images and stereotypes over women themselves is a complex one. At one level individual women may identify with some of the representations but also use them as a fantasy escape from reality or to gain superficial enjoyment whilst remaining cynical about the message. At another level, however, the stereotypes act on groups as a whole so that individuals may only be able to identify themselves in relation to those representations where even non-stereotypical attributes then have to be 'justified' and may give rise to 'guilt'.

Berger's view is that 'Men *act* and women *appear*. Men look at women. Women watch themselves being looked at. This determines not only most relations between men and women but also the relation of women to themselves – she turns herself into an object.' Women in other words, see themselves – through men's eyes – as 'objects' (Berger, 1972, 47).

This view may seem overly deterministic, in line with the 'traditional effects' perspective in media studies, i.e. the assumption that the media affect their audience in a straightforward way. The 'uses and gratifications' perspective, however, assumes that the audience is not passive but is an active partner in the process. The fifth excerpt by Hobson concerns radio listening by women at home and demonstrates the 'use' these women make of that medium without them necessarily accepting the messages. Another important aspect is the *context* in which media consumption takes place. The last extract by Morley considers television viewing within the home and relates it to the other, gendered, processes occurring within the domestic sphere. In attempting to reconcile a deterministic view that assumes totally passive and brainwashed audiences with a view that sees the media as having no influence at all, it might be useful to consider a socio-cultural model of media messages (McQuail, 1983). This view would see the messages not as acting in a straightforward way on individuals but as shaping the knowledge and judgements which individuals and groups acquire which they then may apply, in different ways, in everyday life.

☐ Stereotypes

The definition and use of stereotypes that Perkins lists in this extract illustrate the fact that stereotypes are evaluative descriptions of groups that are socially important in the sense that members of other groups feel the need to be able to describe and conceive of the members of these stereotyped groups in a common, socially acceptable way. The stereotypes only make sense because of shared meanings about the stereotyped group's position, and they use elements of the actual position of the group to produce a simplified picture that allows other people to locate individuals, with particular characteristics, within it.

Reading 1

A stereotype is:

(a) *A group concept:* It describes a group. Personality traits (broadly defined) predominate.
(b) *It is held by a group:* There is a very considerable uniformity about its content. Cannot have a 'private' stereotype.
(c) *Reflects an 'inferior judgemental process':* (but not therefore leading necessarily to an inaccurate conclusion.) Stereotypes short-circuit or block capacity for objective and analytic judgements in favour of well-worn catch-all reactions. To some extent all concepts do this – stereotypes do it to a much greater extent.
(d) (b) and (c) give rise to *simple structure* (mentioned earlier) which frequently conceals complexity (see (e)).
(e) High probability that social stereotypes will be *predominantly evaluative*.
(f) *A concept* – and like other concepts it is a selective, cognitive organising system, and a feature of human thought. . . .

There are stereotypes about:

1. *Major Structural Groups:* colour (black/white); gender (male/female); class (upper/middle/working); age (child/young/adult/old). (Can make jokes about MS groups to mass audience.) *Everybody* is a member of *each* group.
2. *Structurally Significant and Salient Groups:* ethnic groups (Jews/Scots); artists and scientists; mothers-in-law; adolescents in the 1950s. (Comedians' topical jokes mainly from this group.)
3. *Isolated Groups:* social and/or geographic isolation. Gays; American Indians; students in the past; gypsies. (Can't make jokes about this group to mass audience unless it also belongs to another category – probably to *pariah*.)
4. *Pariah Groups:* gays; blacks; Communists in USA?; junkies? (Can make jokes to mass audience – but *may* be 'bad taste' to do so.) Groups here will also belong to another group (1–3).
5. *Opponent Groups:* upper-class twit; male chauvinist pig; reds;

fascists. (Can *sometimes* make jokes to mass audience.) These contrast to others in so far as they are often developed by protesting, deviant or oppressed groups, about their opponents. They can be subdivided into: *counter stereotypes* – e.g. male chauvinist pig – which form part of a counter-ideology and are sufficiently developed to be about a particular group (status and role); and *blanket stereotypes* – which refer to all non-believers – all non-Marxists are fascists; all non-fascists are reds. *Counters* originate from a critical attempt at reinterpretation or re-evaluation (pejorative rather than laudatory) of a dominant group. *Blankets* reinforce group solidarity by claiming a monopoly on knowledge of the 'truth' and grouping all rival claims to 'truth' equally irrelevant and invalid.

6. *Socially/Ideologically Insignificant Groups:* milkmen; redheads

T.E. Perkins, in M. Barrett *et al.*, *Ideology and Cultural Production*, pp. 145–7.

Questions

1. Define, in your own words, a stereotype.
2. Why are women particularly prone to stereotyping?
3. Which of the groups listed in the passage have the most jokes told against them to a mass audience nowadays? Why? Does it change over time?

☐ Reporting Women

Here the TUC is critical of press reportage of certain events involving women. You can no doubt find current examples of your own – but you might also like to consider the extent to which the trade union movement itself is guilty of the stereotypical thinking that it criticises in others.

Reading 2

❝ Anna Ford with her fringe swept away, looked sophisticated and sexy. Her coral pink wrapover dress looked comfortable and as smooth as her interviewing. **❞**

(Daily Mail, January 27)

Breakfast television was launched among a great deal of razzle-dazzle in spring 1983 with the sexual appeal of Ford, Rippon and Scott given some priority by the press. 'Dishy Duel at Dawn' read the headline of the *News of the World* (January 30). Following the trend, the *Sunday Mirror* also spent some time comparing the sexual attributes of the participants. 'Selina Scott, looking like a tired if sexy district nurse, was altogether appealing. So was the pretty little news reader called Debbie Rix who strayed into the studio on the first morning looking as if she was hotfoot from a nightclub, in her figured white satin top'. Guest Susan George 'managed to look sexy at 6.30 am but said nothing of much interest'.

Meanwhile the male weather forecaster, Francis was merely 'cheerful and pleasant'. Over at the TV-AM studios, on the other hand

according to the *Daily Mail* of January 27, 'There was something of a bitchy edge to the expectant air of the TV-AM studios'.

There is hardly any reference to the ability of these women as professionals or their other contributions to the programmes.

The first American woman astronaut in space

When women do hit the headlines in relation to their outstanding achievements, newspapers seem to bend over backwards to trivialise them or to focus on superficial angles. Such was the case of the press treatment of the American astronaut Dr Sally Ride. A cartoon which appeared in the *Daily Star* of June 21, 1983 was typical of much of the coverage at the time. This purported to depict Dr Ride manoeuvring the US spacecraft Challenger and crashing it into a satellite. A rather obvious space-age women drivers' joke.

Peter McKay of the *Daily Mail* could hardly disguise his amazement at NASA insisting on treating Dr Ride 'as one of the boys' at the Kennedy Space Centre, preferring instead a remark made by the American TV personality Johnny Carson that the shuttle launch was to be postponed because Dr Ride could not find a handbag to match her space boots. Dr Ride would not agree to be photographed with her husband (who was not going on the space trip), thus feeding rumours that their marriage was on the rocks, reported McKay.

This was perhaps only topped by the *Daily Express* reporting of the same event. Journalists Michael Richardson and Michael Perry took up considerable column inches in a page lead article speculating on whether or not Dr Ride would take her lipstick in her space-kit! While such treatment is demeaning to Dr Ride and to women generally, it also does not say very much for modern standards of journalism.

TUC, *Images of Inequality: the portrayal of women in the media and advertising.* n/d p. 10

Questions

1. List three elements of female stereotypes portrayed in these passages.
2. Write a version, including headlines, of the introduction of breakfast television and the first woman in space as though the stereotype of women included the features of talent, qualifications, skill and hard work.
3. Find *two* stories in current newspapers that illustrate stereotyped views of the women reported.

□ Washing Whiter

Although static advertisements have received much attention it is the selling that occurs between television programmes that is a daily part of most people's lives. Mamay and Simpson discuss the female roles portrayed in most of the television advertisements they studied and they then tabulate the actions and speech through which the selling is done.

Reading 3

Women's activities in TV commercials fit fairly neatly into three clusters: the *maternal, housekeeping,* and *aesthetic* roles.

Maternal role activities provide care of the family unit or its members. They relate women to all members of their families, not just to children, in a direct personal way. Behaviors such as preparing and serving meals, grocery shopping, laundry, childcare, and care of pets are maternal role activities.

Housekeeping role activities are devoted to care of the interior of the family dwelling and its furniture and equipment. Housekeeping is the care of objects rather than direct services to people, but it is a family-oriented role because the family residence is kept up. Housekeeping includes behaviors such as mopping and waxing floors, dishwashing, dusting, vacuuming, oven cleaning, and toilet bowl cleaning.

The aesthetic role is individualistic. It relates the woman minimally, if at all, to her family. The main type of aesthetic role activity seen in commercials concerns beautification or hygiene of the user of a product. Most ads for bath soap, shampoo, makeup, and women's clothing stress the products' aesthetic qualities, not their utilitarian value or their price. The usual image is that beauty and cleanliness are ends in themselves, directly giving the woman a sense of well-being, rather than having the purpose of pleasing her husband or another person. A second type of aesthetic role commercial employs a sensuous woman as a sex object to entice men to buy things.

Action Patterns by Female Role

		Action pattern: Percent of commercials[1]							
Female role	n	Woman uses	Woman talks	Man uses	Man talks	Two women talk	Man and woman talk	Voice-over Male	Female
Maternal	160	31.3	25.6	10.0	14.4	5.0	14.4	60.6	8.1
Housekeeping	65	44.6	30.8	21.5	12.3	10.8	41.5	55.4	1.5
Aesthetic	82	46.3	53.7	1.2	9.8	12.2	8.5	46.3	14.6
All roles	307	38.1	34.2	10.1	12.7	8.1	18.6	55.7	8.5

[1]Percentages add to more than 100 because some commercials showed more than one action pattern.

D. Mamay and L. Simpson, *Sex Roles*, Vol. 7, No. 12, pp. 1224–5.

Questions

1. Which of women's roles is most often portrayed in the commercials studied? Why do you think this is the case?
2. Why are male voices more often used for 'voice overs'?
3. Name some current commercials on television that utilise the
   (a) maternal
   (b) housekeeping
   (c) aesthetic
   roles of women.

☐ Femininity Again

If the culture of romance pervades magazines aimed at girls and young women, once adult status has been achieved the culture of femininity is portrayed in women's magazines – mainly with reference to the roles of mother, wife and beautifier. Magazines, of course, are an important vehicle for advertising, and to some extent articles and advertisements reinforce each other.

Reading 4

Women's magazines collectively comprise a social institution which serves to foster and maintain a cult of femininity. This cult is manifested both as a social group to which all those born female can belong, and as a set of practices and beliefs: rites and rituals, sacrifices and ceremonies, whose periodic performance re-affirms a common femininity and shared group membership. In promoting a cult of femininity these journals are not merely reflecting the female role in society; they are also supplying one source of definitions of, and socialisation into, that role.

Instruction, encouragement and entertainment to do with the business of being a woman are directed at specific client/target groups such as housewives, younger women, mothers, brides and slimmers. By fostering this learning process through the messages disseminated by their editors, or high priestesses, the cult's oracles help to sustain the faithful in their beliefs, and to attract new followers to worship its totem: Woman herself. In maintaining the desire of adherents new and old to perfect and display their femininity, these journals can be seen to fulfil another of their most enduring purposes – the creation of profits for their owners in a market where the few organisations own the many titles.

To state that women's magazines promote a cult of femininity is to state more than the economic truism that they do this to maximise profits. A larger and more circular process is at work. By identifying the female sex aged 15 and over as their main target group, women's magazines promote the market importance of that sex and thereby confer status on women as a group, and make womanly things a serious business. They provide a public platform and a symbolic social order which consistently offers a woman a cheap and accessible source of positive evaluation, alongside practical directions for fulfilling her potential as a cultist – and as a consumer. They consciously set out to foster a woman's sense of her own worth – at a fraction of the cost of alternative sources of therapy such as psychoanalysis or plastic surgery, available only to the privileged few.

They also preach the ideal of a woman's power of self-determination. They do this through their overwhelming emphasis on self-help. Putting Samual Smiles into petticoats, they proclaim self-help as the doctrine of salvation for all areas of woman's life from the most public to the most private. This ethic is harnessed to the specific aspirations that they set concerning female achievement and fulfilment. These aspirations are to do with the whole range of tasks, goals, and obligations inherent in becoming a woman. 'True' feminine fulfilment and personal happiness are found through achieving these material and emotional ends.

Women's magazines also provide the syllabus and step-by-step instructions which help to socialise their readers into the various ages and stages of the demanding – but rewarding – state of womanhood. Novices are led through the appropriate attitudes, rituals and purchases to achieve their chosen ends of *femme fatale*, super cook or office boss. In following their leaders, individual women help to produce and maintain a cult of femininity which has potent, if unintended, consequences for women as a group, apart from their quite specific intended, commercial aims and consequences.

M. Ferguson, *Forever Feminine: Women's Magazines and the Cult of Femininity*, pp., 184–5.

Questions

1. Explain and discuss what you understand by 'the cult of femininity to which all females belong'.
2. To what extent do you agree that women's magazines foster a sense of self-worth? How do magazines attempt to do this?
3. List the ways in which you think women's magazines influence women as consumers.

☐ Women's Use of the Media

From her study of wives at home, Hobson shows the important functions that radio performs to alleviate their particular circumstances, regardless of the messages and stereotypes being broadcast.

Reading 5

The housewives in this study do listen to Radio 1 and find the experience enjoyable. The radio, for the most part, is listened to during the day while they are engaged in domestic labour, housework and child care. As Anne said, 'It's on in the background all the time'. In some cases switching on the radio is part of the routine of beginning the day; it is, in fact, the first *boundary* in the working day. In terms of the 'structurelessness' of the experience of housework, the time boundaries provided by radio are important in the women's own division of their time. . . .

The constant reference to time during the programmes on Radio 1 also helps to structure the time sequences of the work which women perform while they listen to the radio. Programmes are self-definitional, as *The Breakfast Show, Mid-morning Programme*, which includes *Coffee Break* at 11 a.m. At the time of the study Tony Blackburn was running the morning show (9 a.m.–12 noon), in which he had the 'Tiny Tots' spot at 11 a.m., during which a record was played for children and Blackburn attempted to teach a nursery rhyme to the children listening while the 'mums' had a coffee break. During David Hamilton's afternoon programme (2 p.m.–5 p.m.) the 'Tea at Three' spot is included, when once more women are encouraged to 'put their feet up'. The disc jockeys (DJs) use points of reference within the expected daily routines of their listeners, and some of these references are responded to by the women in the study. The programmes which are listened to are Radio 1 and BRMB local radio, the former being the more popular. Responses to questions about radio are always given in terms of the disc jockey who introduces the programme, with the records referred to in a secondary capacity. . . .

Within the overall picture of isolation which has emerged in the lives of the women in this study, the disc jockey can be seen as having the function of providing the missing 'company' of another person in the lives of the women. . . .

The disc jockey, as well as providing relief from isolation, links the isolated individual woman with the knowledge that there are others in the same position. Similarly, this can be seen as a functional effect of 'phone-in' programmes. One of the women says: 'I like listening to the people that phone in. I like the conversations . . . I suppose it's 'cos I'm on me own.' These programmes not only provide contact with the 'outside' world; they also reinforce the privatized isolation by reaffirming the consensual position – there are thousands of other women in the same situation, in a sort of 'collective isolation'. . . .

Radio can be seen, then, as providing women with a musical reminder of their leisure activities before they married. It also, as they say, keeps them up to date with new records. Since they do not have any spare money to buy records, this is an important way in which they can listen to music. Since listening to music and dancing are the leisure activities which they would most like to pursue, radio is also a substitute for the real world of music and discos which they have lost. Also, it provides a crucial relief from their isolation. The chatter of the disc jockey may appear inane and trivial, but the popularity of radio, both in national and local terms and in the responses of the women in this study, would appear to suggest that it fulfils certain functions in providing music to keep them 'happy and on the move'. Radio creates its own audience through its constant reference to forthcoming programmes and items within programmes, . . . the women in this study do appear to regard Radio 1 as a friend, and they certainly view the disc jockeys as important means of negotiating or managing the tensions caused by the isolation in their lives.

D. Hobson, in S. Hall *et al.*, *Culture, Media, Language*, pp. 105–9.

Questions

1. Are the time boundaries provided by radio important to women at home? Give reasons for your answer.
2. Which two functions does the author maintain that the D.J. serves for these listeners?
3. What other purpose(s) are served by radio programmes?

□ Watching With One Eye

The last extract was about women's relationship to a medium when they were on their own primarily doing other things. This passage on television viewing within the household illustrates the different meanings that the house usually has for women and men, the domestic power relations that determine the whole group's use of the medium and men's ambivalence to certain aspects of their participation.

Reading 6

There is one fundamental point which needs to be made concerning the basically different positioning of men and women within the domestic sphere. . . . The essential point here is that the dominant model of gender relations within this society (and certainly within that sub-section of it represented in my sample) is one in which the home is primarily defined for men as a site of leisure – in distinction to the 'industrial time' of their employment outside the home – while the home is primarily defined for women as a sphere of work (whether or not they also work outside the home). This simply means that in investigating television viewing in the home one is by definition investigating something which men are better placed to do whole-heartedly, and which women seem only to be able to do distractedly and guiltily, because of their continuing sense of their domestic responsibilities. Moreover, this differential positioning is given a greater significance as the home becomes increasingly defined as the 'proper' sphere of leisure, with the decline of public forms of entertainment and the growth of home-based leisure technologies such as video, etc. . . .

Masculine power is evident in a number of the families as the ultimate determinant on occasions of conflict over viewing choices ('we discuss what we all want to watch and the biggest wins. That's me. I'm the biggest', Man, Family 4). More crudely, it is even more apparent in the case of those families who have an automatic control device. None of the women in any of the families use the automatic control regularly. A number of them complain that their husbands use the channel control device obsessively, channel flicking across programmes when their wives are trying to watch something else. Characteristically, the control device is the symbolic possession of the father (or of the son, in the father's absence) which sits 'on the arm of Daddy's chair' and is used almost exclusively by him. It is a highly visible symbol of condensed power relations. . . .

One major finding is the consistency of the distinction between the characteristic ways in which men and women describe their viewing activity. Essentially the men state a clear preference for viewing attentively, in silence, without interruption 'in order not to miss any-thing'. Moreover, they display puzzlement at the way their wives and daughters watch television. This the women themselves describe as a fundamentally social activity, involving ongoing conversation, and usually the performance of at least one domestic activity (ironing, etc.) at the same time. Indeed, many of the women feel that just to watch television without doing anything else at the same time would be an indefensible waste of time, given their sense of their domestic obligations. To watch in this way is something they rarely do, except occasionally, when alone or with other women friends, when they have managed to construct an 'occasion' on which to watch their favourite programme, video or film. The women note that their hus-bands are always 'on at them' to shut up. The men can't really understand how their wives can follow the programmes if they are doing something else at the same time. . . .

It is the men, on the whole, who speak of checking through the paper (or the teletext) to plan their evening's viewing. Very few of the women seem to do this at all, except in terms of already knowing which evenings and times their favourite series are on and thus not needing to check the schedule. This is also an indication of a different attitude to viewing as a whole. Many of the women have a much more take-it-or-leave-it attitude, not caring much if they miss things (except for their favourite serials). . . .

Women seem to show much less reluctance to 'admit' that they talk about television to their friends and workmates. Very few men admit to doing this. It is as if they feel that to admit that they watch too much television (especially with the degree of involvement that would be implied by finding it important enough to talk about) would be to put their very masculinity in question. The only standard exception is where the men are willing to admit that they talk about sport on television. All this is clearly related to the theme of gender and programme choice and the 'masculinity/femininity' syllogism identified there. Some part of this is simply to do with the fact that femininity is a more expressive cultural mode than is masculinity. Thus even if women watch less, with less intent viewing styles, none the less they are inclined to talk about television *more* than men despite the fact that the men watch more of it, more attentively. . . .

The issue of the differential tendency for women and men to talk about their television viewing is of considerable interest. . . .

In principle it could be argued that the claims many of the male respondents make about only watching 'factual' television are a misrepresentation of their actual behaviour, based on their anxiety about admitting to watching fictional programmes. However, even if this were the case, it would remain a social fact of some interest that the male respondents felt this compulsion to misrepresent their actual behaviour in this particular way. Moreover, this very reluctance to talk about some of the programmes they may watch itself has important consequences. Even if it were the case that men and women in fact watched the same range of programmes (contrary to the accounts they gave me), the fact that the men are reluctant to talk about watching anything other than factual programmes or sport means that their viewing experience is profoundly different from that of the women in the sample. Given that meanings are made not simply in the moment of individual viewing, but also in the subsequent social processes of discussion and 'digestion' of material viewed, the men's much greater reluctance to talk about (part of) their viewing will mean that their consumption of television material is of a quite different kind from that of their wives.

D. Morley, *Family Television: Cultural Power and Domestic Leisure*, pp. 147–58.

Questions

1. How does the author relate gender patterns within the household to different styles of television viewing?
2. Why are men, according to this passage, more reluctant to discuss television programmes than women?
3. 'Men's consumption of television material is of a quite different kind from that of their wives.' Do you agree? If so, why? If not, why not?

Essay Questions

1. 'Sexism is a most noticeable feature of nearly all the output of the mass media.' Discuss this statement in the light of sociological evidence. (AEB 1985)
2. To what extent are the stereotypes of women as portrayed in the media important in influencing both men and women?
3. Explain the nature and purpose of stereotypes with regard to women.
4. 'Women use and understand the media differently from men.' Discuss.

Further Reading

L. Broadbent *et al.* (Glasgow Media Group), *War and Peace News*. Chapter 3 is an analysis of the way families and women associated with the troops sent to the Falklands dispute were portrayed. Detailed and interesting.

M. Ferguson, *Forever Feminine: Women's Magazines and the Cult of Femininity*. A study of *Woman*, *Woman's Own* and *Woman's Weekly* between 1949 and 1980 illustrating the changes and similarities over thirty years.

D. Hobson, 'Housewives and the mass media', in S. Hall *et al.*, *Culture, Media and Language*. Fascinating sociological account of the relationship of homebound women to radio and television programmes.

J. King and M. Stott, *Is this your life? Images of Women in the Media*. There are chapters in this book on women's magazines, radio, films, newspapers, television, advertising and so on. It is not a sociology book, as the contributors are all women working in the areas they write about, but it contains a lot of factual and interesting information. Easy to read.

T. Perkins, 'Rethinking stereotypes', in M. Barrett *et al.*, *Ideology and Cultural Production*. More advanced reading for those who feel able to tackle it: worthwhile struggling as it is an excellent sociological discussion of the concept.

D. Souhami, *A Woman's Place: The Changing Picture of Women in Britain*. Not sociological, but the chapter on image stereotyping has some good photographs and interesting tit-bits of information.

J. Winship, 'A woman's world: *Woman* – an ideology of femininity', in Women's Studies Group CCCS, *Women Take Issue*. A sociological study of *Woman* magazine.

7 | Formal politics and trades unions

At the turn of the twentieth century women did not even have a parliamentary vote, and they had a long struggle to obtain full citizenship. Yet women's participation in trades unions and radical politics earlier this century was crucial to the development of the modern Labour Party. Politics is about power, which is concerned with the control and allocation of resources. One aspect of power is that powerful groups are able to prevent other groups from raising issues that are not in the interests of the power holders. Thus, issues that are important to women do not often form part of the debate or the basis of policies. Another important point is that formal politics is part of the public, as opposed to the private, sphere and contains the activities that are defined as 'more important', yet this public arena is less responsive to women than men, and this is important to remember when discussing women's participation in this sphere.

Focusing on political parties and trades unions, in any case, implies a narrow definition of politics; other activities affect policies and women may be better represented in these other activities – ad hoc and protest groups, for example, as we shall see in Chapter 8. In this respect women do have a long history of participation; they were prominent in the eighteenth-century food riots and the nineteenth-century demonstrations against the Poor Law. Women have also played an active role in revolutionary movements, for example, in Britain in the seventeenth century, France in the eighteenth, Russia in the twentieth and in some countries in South America. Nationalist movements around the world have also contained high proportions of women.

With regard to political participation in terms of voting in Britain it is often asserted that women are more 'Conservative' than men. The first table, from Siltanen and Stanworth, shows the figures for the 1979 election in Britain and you can decide for yourself to what extent this is true. An important point in the information is the age-range in relation to voting patterns. The second extract by Randall points out the features of public politics that are not conducive to women's participation, and she sees this as the issue rather than the fact that women are 'uninterested' in politics as is often assumed.

Male dominance in formal political systems seems to be universal but the degree of dominance does vary as the table in the third extract by Norris illustrates. Even when women do become members of elite political groups they are usually assigned to specialities considered 'appropriate' for women's concerns. In most countries these women are located in the ministries and departments of culture, health and welfare – positions usually carrying less power and prestige than positions dealing with foreign policy, budgets and defence. In the third extract some of the cultural, socioeconomic and political factors that are important in women's lack of representation at the higher levels of formal politics are discussed.

Although neither women nor their interests are well represented in the political arena, nevertheless women are deeply affected by the policy outcomes of the political process, and the state is important not only in maintaining systems in which women are subordinate but also in regulating and defining their behaviour. In Chapter 2 the role of the state in defining and regulating the family, marriage and parenthood was discussed; sexuality and fertility are also controlled through the availability of birth control, abortion and policies on sexual violence. Even the Equal Pay Act (1970) and the Sex Discrimination Act (1975), which appear to be women-centred policies, assume that the struggle for equality is an individual one waged by women who are able to perceive discrimination and bring a formal charge; which, if they win, affects only them and not the category of women or female employees to which they belong. Policies are conceived, directed and implemented by men. The fourth extract by Pascall focuses on housing policy to illustrate the assumptions about women's role that underpin both the design of houses and town planning. Other policies on everyday aspects of life can be dissected in the same way to show how policies that women have little part in framing, in turn frame them.

Trades Unions are also public groups in which women are underrepresented but whose policies affect not only their employment prospects but also their home life, as illustrated in Chapter 6. During the nineteenth century women succeeded in setting up women's societies for their employment protection and in 1875 the first woman to enter the TUC was Emma Paterson, who then opposed protective legislation on the grounds that it was degrading to women to be classified with children and would reduce their earning power. Local women's unions sprang up but they were short-lived and had financial difficulties, so in 1906 the National Federation of Women Workers was formed, run by Mary Macarthur who is mentioned in the excerpt by Godwin. The fifth extract by Drake was written in 1921; she discusses the reasons why trades unions had an interest in restricting women's employment. The sixth extract, by Godwin, is an account of a women's strike in 1910 to show that, contrary to popular opinion, women have a long history of organising to protect their earnings and employment rights – often at great personal cost. Besides activities on these issues women in the Labour movement were also, at this time, concerned about social and welfare provision such as school meals and medical services.

The seventh extract by Coote and Campbell discusses the extent to which unions have fulfilled their potential for improving the position of women. It might be illuminating to consider whether any of the factors that made unions less than keen to support women earlier this century, as discussed by Drake, still apply. The last table, in showing the female membership of some of the largest trades unions and the proportion of women at higher levels, may be helpful in explaining why change has been so slow.

□ **Conservative Women?**

Voting statistics are the basis for the contention that women are more likely than men to vote Conservative. If, however, the age factor is taken into account there may be reasons other than the 'nature' of women themselves that account for such patterns.

Reading 1

Women and voting in Britain. Sex difference by age and party vote, 1979 (percentage of total sample)

Age	Sex	Conservative	Labour	Liberal
20–9	Men	25	27	21
	Women	30	30	13
30–59	Men	39	32	11
	Women	41	33	12
60–75	Men	40	36	8
	Women	46	32	10
Over 75	Men	40	26	12
	Women	52	18	3

J. Siltanen and M. Stanworth, *Women and the Public Sphere*, p. 139.

Questions

1. Describe the female and male patterns of voting shown in the table.
2. What factors might account for the differences between women and men shown in the table?
3. Would you expect the pattern to change over time? Give reasons for your answer.

□ Public Politics

The problem of women's participation in politics is crucially affected by the fact that formal politics are part of the 'public' arena. Political institutions are 'masculine' in their operation, their assumptions, and the issues thought to be important and it is these factors, rather than women's 'personalities', that explain the patterns of participation and representation.

Reading 2

Politics is a public activity. In communities where there is no real distinction between private and public, between the life of the family and a transcending community, politics as a distinctively conscious activity of decision-making on behalf of the community is likely to be at a minimum. As politics has emerged as an aspect of social organisation, so has some kind of demarcation between the private, non-political sphere and the public. . . .

I am suggesting that, leaving aside questions of the character of specific political institutions, their very location within a non-domestic sphere makes participation more difficult for women than for men. This obstacle, paradoxically, increases, assuming that family roles remain largely unchanged, in societies with highly differentiated processes for public participation. Consequently, women have many ways of exercising informal political influence when politics is less institutionalised and may prefer, in more institutionalised political systems, to participate in *ad hoc* or even protest politics. . . .

Political institutions can be uninviting to women. Simply because they have been until recently exclusively male, because men still dominate their leadership positions, women are discouraged. Then also male dominance tends to generate a 'masculine' style and atmosphere. Political scientists often specify the behaviour traits, not commonly associated with women, that effective political participation in contemporary democratic politics requires. Sometimes the activist is depicted as rational in the sense of being able logically to relate ends and means. The stereotypical woman of course is not rational, in this sense, but emotional, at best intuitive. Alternatively the activist is expected to be adult and responsible, in contrast to women's alleged dependence and immaturity. Finally a less idealistic version of democratic politics requires the participant to be competitive and aggressive, again the opposite of women's supposed passivity. Of these three attributes – rationality, responsibility and aggressiveness – it is the third which feminists (including myself) may be most prepared to accept as a prerequisite for effective participation in contemporary politics and to agree is a trait currently exhibited less by women than by men. Moreover, within male-dominated political institutions, women may be facing not only a competitive style, but also male hostility directed specifically, if half-consciously, at them as intruders.

Then again, such institutions will function in ways practically convenient to the men who established and run them. Considerations such as where, when and how often meetings are held will be more serious deterrents to élite political participation but may also constrain participation at grassroots level.

Finally, it is frequently suggested that politics, as presently practised, focuses on issues that are peripheral to women's interests; women lack a 'stake' in the subject matter of conventional politics. This argument can only be accepted with reservations. Issues such as defence, foreign policy and economic policy clearly are of urgent relevance to men and women alike. What is more true is that conventional politics tends to neglect or to label as 'administrative', 'social' or 'cultural', issues that are of most immediate concern to many women, such as nursery school provision, or standards of housing or education. This is one reason for women's participation in community action.

The pattern of women's political participation cannot, in conclusion, simply be explained by reference to their personality, practical situation or even distribution within the social system. Features of conventional politics themselves act as deterrents. It is in this context that the appeal of women's associations, of 'unconventional' political participation and of women's liberation, becomes so easy to understand.

V. Randall, *Women and Politics*, pp. 66–8.

Questions

1. Why can political institutions be 'uninviting to women'?
2. To what extent do you agree with the author that aggressiveness is a prerequisite for effective participation in contemporary politics?
3. What social effects do women's lack of representation and participation in formal politics have?

☐ Political Elites

The table shows a huge discrepancy between countries with regard to the percentage of women in their national legislatures. This passage discusses the structures and processes that inhibit women from achieving political office. The structures and processes clearly combine in different ways for different countries, so giving women more or less chance depending on their nationality.

Reading 3

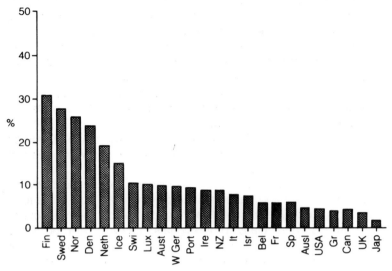

Women in national legislatures, 1983

Cultural attitudes may play an important role in the three hurdles candidates have to cross to achieve office, since women must be willing to stand, they must be judged suitable candidates by the party selectorate and they must be given support by the voters. If attitudes towards female candidates are negative, this could be expected to influence the number of women who want to run for office, who feel that it would be an appropriate vocation and who think that they would stand a chance. As potential candidates, the selectorate may judge their electoral prospects to be doubtful and therefore may be reluctant to nominate them, even if they do not share the public's values.

Lastly, in a direct way public attitudes could be reflected in the vote which female candidates attract, where considerations to gender override other factors like partisanship. This suggests that cultural attitudes might be significant, yet the matter is complex since countries which are often perceived as relatively traditional, such as Switzerland and Ireland, have double the number of women in office to the United States, where the second-wave women's movement might have been expected to have most impact on sex-role attitudes.

Alternative research suggests that a major role is played by *socio-economic factors*, especially the proportion of women in a country who are eligible for office by virtue of their economic and educational experience. The selectorate will only nominate candidates for office who have certain qualifications, increasingly requiring formal educational credentials. As a number of studies have found university qualifications distinguish élites from non-élites throughout the world. Compared with the population, university graduates are statistically overrepresented in legislative élites, roughly ten or twenty to one. Education, as well as qualifying candidates to be nominated in the eyes of the selectorate, might also be important in motivating candidates to stand. . . .

This suggests that as the socio-economic experience of women changes they will gain the necessary qualifications which lead to positions in political élites.

Certain studies also suggest a significant connection between female recruitment and patterns of employment. Political élites tend to be dominated by representatives from a small number of occupational groups, particularly professionals. Lawyers are politically prominent almost everywhere; they usually make up 15 to 25 per cent of national legislators, rising to half of all representatives in America. Journalists, academics, teachers and businessmen are also overrepresented in parliaments compared with their numbers in the population. These groups often lend practitioners skills which are useful in elected office, such as expertise and confidence in public speaking, knowledge of government and familiarity with the law. These jobs also allow considerable flexibility so that professionals can combine a long-term career with the demands and uncertainties of office, while this may be more difficult for workers in manual jobs or middle management. . . . The high status of these jobs may influence selectorates when choosing candidates. . . .

In so far as there are few women in these occupations, they are at a clear disadvantage in standing for office under present circumstances. As increasing numbers of women enter such professions as law, the media and business, this may place more on the traditional ladder leading to political office. . . . Alternatively, others emphasise the significance of *political factors*, with the parties playing a crucial role as 'gatekeepers' to office. One of the primary functions of political parties is to nominate and support suitable candidates for office. . . .

Amongst political variables a number of recent studies stress the importance of voting systems, arguing that elections with proportional representation using the party list system give women a stronger chance of being nominated and elected than simple majority systems. This is supported by evidence which shows that countries with first-past-the-post systems, such as Canada and Britain, have only a handful of women in parliament, while female representation is generally stronger in countries using proportional representation. Yet it is unclear why there are significant differences between countries which share a similar electoral system such as Belgium and Denmark or Israel and the Netherlands. It is also unclear how far the introduction of proportional representation would by itself improve the political position of women. This suggests the need to analyse the relative influence of voting systems compared with other factors as elections only function within a broader context.

P. Norris, *Politics and Sexual Equality*, pp. 115–24.

Questions

1. Why might cultural attitudes be an important determinant of the number of women to achieve political office?
2. Which socio-economic factors does the author describe as being important in explaining the lack of women in political elites?
3. How important are political factors in explaining the number of women who achieve political office?
4. Attempt to explain the differences in the percentage of women in national legislatures shown in the table.

☐ The Outcome of Politics is Policy

Housing policy is used here to illustrate the assumptions about women that have shaped policies in this area and the impact that these policies now have on women. Both owner-occupation and public housing are provided on a basis that discriminates against non-nuclear 'units' without men. The planning of where houses should be located helps to reinforce the structures that exist, and houses themselves are designed not for the structure of the population as it exists, nor the way that many people want to live, but on an idealised form of household.

Reading 4

Owner-occupation has dominated housing policy in the postwar period. Privately rented accommodation has declined severely. Waves of public sector building have produced a significant public stock; but council house sales, demolition of structurally deficient developments, and recent public expenditure policy have drastically restricted access here for new tenants. Thus owner-occupation has grown to nearly two-thirds of the total housing stock.

Access to owner-occupation depends, of course, upon income. It is available, therefore, to better-off men and to women largely through men. Women without men are much less likely to be able to buy houses. Although the number of successful women mortgage applicants has gone up, in 1981 the proportion of females to males was still only 1:10 in the UK. . . . Thus women without men have limited access to owner-occupation. Access is largely through men and preferably through being part of a 'building-society-preferred' couple. Limited access matters to women whose marriages break down, as well as to those choosing to live outside marriage. A policy relying on owner-occupation thus has particular significance for women. The decline of the privately rented sector – once the resort of those outside 'standard families' – has severely cut back housing access for women alone and women with children. Local authority policies are now crucial for women without men. Alternative options have withered away.

Housing policy within the public sector, therefore, needs examination. Detailed practice is decentralized and hard to document. However, there are two main stages at which local authority preferences for 'standard families' may be felt. The first is selection of households for council housing; the second is allocation to particular properties. On the first point, waiting lists which stress length of residence and allocate points according to family size tend to tell against women alone with children (because they tend to move often and lack one adult member compared with other families), and virtually to exclude women alone (unless they are elderly). . . .

Both allocation and building policies in the public sector have favoured two-parent families with children (with special housing for the elderly a rather recent exception). Thus they have largely excluded single people and have disadvantaged one-parent families. Since poorer people – including most women without men – depend very largely on the public sector, and since housing is one of the fundamentals for any kind of living, public sector housing policies are a powerful conditioning factor in women's lives.

The shape of the 'standard family' is suggested by the shape of the 'standard dwelling'. The overwhelming preponderance is of two- or three-bedroom units in both public (80 per cent) and owner-occupied (86 per cent) sectors. The dwelling is likely to be a house, semi-detached, terraced, or detached (in that order). A higher proportion of local authority units are one-bedroom (reflecting the priority given to elderly people) and flats (30 per cent), reflecting high-rise policies in the 1960s. Apart from a small minority of 'special needs' housing, such as warden-assisted flats, the emphasis is on self-containment, rather than on shared or communal facilities. . . .

If housing design reflects an ideology of female domesticity, the shape of cities puts domesticity in its place. Its place is to be separate from public life. Increasingly, the structure and organization of cities reflect the sexual division of labour in concrete form. Housing estates, garden cities, and suburbs segregate domestic life; they ensure its privacy, its disconnection from the public world of work and politics. . . .

In segregating domestic from public life, the shape of cities also helps to segregate women from public life. Men may bridge the gap between the two worlds, daily travelling to work, retreating to a haven of rest. But for women home is work as well as (sometimes) haven. Women who must be at the school gate, or keep an eye on elderly relatives, women who have work to do in the haven, cannot so easily divide their lives.

G. Pascall, *Social Policy: A Feminist Analysis*, Tavistock, pp. 133–8.

Questions

1. What are the main features of housing policy described?
2. How does this policy discriminate against women?
3. What assumptions about women's role underpin house design and planning?
4. Which particular aspects of conventional house design would you change to suit other ways of living from those assumed at present?

☐ Trades Unions in the Past

As this passage was written in 1921 you may find the language a bit quaint! But it contains sharp accusations against the male trades unions of the time and is a reminder that women have long understood, and been able to articulate, their social condition.

Reading 5

Trade union restrictions on female labour are the common rule in organized trades. According as the men's trade unions are strong, female labour is entirely prohibited – any future, if not the present, generation of workers – or women are restricted to certain inferior branches of the industry, or to certain unorganized districts. Variations of policy are mainly determined by circumstance, and a total absence of restrictions does not necessarily argue a difference of principle. Where women's employment is an established fact before organization begins, and men have no means of preventing it, restrictions are obviously useless. A genuine indifference to lines of sex demarcation is practically confined to cotton weavers.

This widespread character of trade union restrictions on female labour points to a common cause or causes. Men trade unionists are accused of a policy of sex privilege and prejudice, especially by middle-class women. The charge, unfortunately, has a basis of truth. A belief in the divine right of every man to his job is not peculiar to kings or capitalists, and democracy is hard to practice at home. The comparatively favourable working conditions enjoyed by men in organized trades have been mainly built up by their own exertions in the past, and they are not disposed to share these advantages with a new host of women competitors. Trade unionists are, in fact, no better than other men. A more respectable motive, but one not less keenly resented by women, is the anxiety sometimes expressed by men to protect women-folk from harm, and to confine them, if not to the home, at least to 'womanly' occupations. Men's claim so to dictate to women their manner of employment has at no time been admitted by women trade unionists, who maintain as jealously as men their right to earn their living in their own way. Least of all are women prepared to accept men's judgment in matters of health and morals; and they are not a little suspicious of a 'chivalry' which may deliberately prohibit them from operations 'within the capacity of a child,' and yet expressly allow them 'to carry loads about the work-shop!' At Trades Union Congresses, the National Federation of Women Workers has more than once protested against men's interference in the matter of 'unsuitable' occupations, and its members have urged that this question, which is chiefly a medical one, should be referred for enquiry to a responsible Government commission. As a matter of fact, women's claim to earn their living in their own way is not at present seriously disputed by men trade unionists, who realize that a policy of sex privilege and prejudice can only lead to the damage of their own cause, and obscure the real issue. The true causes of trade union restrictions on female labour are economic. From a long and bitter experience, trade unionists have learned that the introduction of women into men's trades is invariably followed by a fall of wages from the men's to a women's level, so that men are finally driven from employment. . . . Nor did the experience of the war, and the general failure of 'substituted' women to secure men's wages, incline men to change their opinion. It served on the contrary to rally women in support of the men's policy. It is significant that the only opposition to the Restoration of Pre-War Practices Act came from middle-class women's organizations.

B. Drake, *Women in Trade Unions*, pp. 220–1.

Questions

1. Why, according to the author, did trades unions restrict women's employment?
2. Why might women have been suspicious of 'chivalry'?
3. Do any of the factors discussed by the author still hold true?

□ A Penny an Hour

Earlier this century many women were employed for poverty wages and their conditions of work were appalling. The Women's Federation, led by Mary Macarthur, achieved some successes for these women. But going on strike and forgoing the only income available to them was a serious business, not undertaken lightly, for women such as these chainmakers.

Reading 6

But at the time a further great battle had to be fought. Chainmaking, notorious in the Black Country for low wages for women, was one of the four Boards first set up and, in May 1910, a rate of 2½d per hour was fixed. This meant nothing to the men. They had been organised by an able local leader, Tom Fitch, into a strong union and tolerable rates and conditions had been secured. The situation of the women was very different. They worked for the most part on small forges set up in sheds and outhouses in their own backyards, finding their own fuel and tools and earning at best 7s to 8s a week; 5s to 6s was usual.

The new rates meant big increases for women but the firms within the Employers' Association were prepared to pay; not so the many employers and middlemen who were outside the Association. They used the six months delay provided in the Act as an opportunity to pile up stocks, and persuaded many women, too ignorant to realise what they were doing, to contract out of the Act using the threat that otherwise they would get no work. Mary Macarthur decided that if employers could so frustrate the purpose of the Act, no Trade Board would be safe. Two things, she said, must be done; first, the good employers must give firm undertakings to pay the rate, which they did; second, the cheated women must strike. It was a desperate move, for the women would be penniless.

Much credit for handling the strike must go to the woman on the spot, Julia Varley. She set up an influential local committee to collect funds and embarked on some inspired publicity. She brought the women out from their back streets into the prosperous centre of Birmingham, hung with their chains and with placards bearing the words, 'Britain's disgrace, 1*d* an hour'. She said that the women who paraded were between 60 and 90 years of age. She took them to the Annual Congress of the TUC and on to the platform, silently raising their chained hands. The effect can be imagined. For all that, it was a bitter struggle and lasted ten weeks before the employers capitulated and the women returned to work, with wages doubled in some cases.

A. Godwin, in L. Middleton (ed.), *Women in the Labour Movement*, pp. 100–1.

Questions

1. Find another example of a woman's strike in the twentieth century and discuss the factors that helped it to succeed or fail.
2. Consider the similarities and differences between a contemporary women's strike and your earlier example.
3. Has occupational change made strikes by women more or less likely? Give reasons for your answer.

□ Plus ça Change?

Socialist and marxist feminists have viewed trades unions as important institutions where men can support women in their struggle for equality. In describing the activities of modern unions Coote and Campbell are, however, disappointed by how little has been achieved. Radical feminists would, though, expect men – even trades unionists – to put their own interests first. Trade union activity is thus important sociologically in pointing to relationships of gender and class.

Reading 7

In 1961 there were four male trade unionists for every female union member. By 1980, the ratio dropped to barely two-to-one. Female membership increased during that period by 110 per cent – more than twice the rate at which women joined the labour force (an increase of 48.5 per cent). Within the same years, the number of men in the workforce remained fairly stable, while they increased their union membership by only 17.6 per cent.

The unions have held out considerable promise. They have power in the workplace. They have a hot-line to government (under Labour, at least). Their business is to represent workers and help them to win better pay, benefits and conditions. The British trade union movement is perhaps the most experienced and influential in the Western capitalist world. Through the unions, women have a chance to enlist male support in order to fight with them, rather than fighting alone. . . .

For some groups of women, unions have negotiated a real improvement in their basic wages, relative to men's. But the overall gap between female and male take-home pay has narrowed by less than ten pence in ten years. The extent to which women's jobs are segregated from men's has increased during the 1970s. And there is evidence that the trade unions have in some instances deterred women from pursuing claims under the new 'equality legislation'. The laws were intended to compensate for past failures of collective bargaining: had the unions succeeded in negotiating adequate pay and conditions for their female members, there might have been no need for Parliament to step in. The unions backed the campaign for legislation, but at the time many trade unions argued that the laws were an unnecessary intrusion into their own territory: wages and conditions were a matter for collective bargaining: they did not want the autonomy of the unions undermined by courts or tribunals or quangos: and anyway the laws wouldn't work. . . .

As the economic crisis deepened, the unions became increasingly preoccupied with saving their members' jobs and defending the purchasing power of wages. Nobody came out into the open and *said* that men's interests should be looked after first; but it was widely accepted among trade unionists that the fight against female disadvantage was not a top priority in a period of recession. Nurseries have been closed down, maternity rights have been curtailed. A higher proportion of women than men joined the dole queue in eight out of ten years between 1970 and 1980. But although some unions have voiced a protest, defensive action in these areas has been negligible. It seems that women's economic equality has to be a no-cost benefit, which can only be sanctioned in a period of economic growth, because redistribution of wealth between women and men is not seriously considered.

The most obvious cause of the failure to improve the lot of women is that women themselves still have no real power in their unions. They have little or no control over the making or implementation of policy. They are still severely under-represented on their unions' executive committees, among full-time officials and on delegations to the TUC. . . .

It isn't just that women have failed to fill key posts in the unions; they have remained absent from a whole range of union activities . . .

There are no formal bars to female participation and there are few overt acts of discrimination against women. So we need to look deeper – at the history of trade unionism, at the structure of paid and unpaid labour, and at the way these have shaped the different traditions and attitudes of female and male workers.

A. Coote and B. Campbell, *Sweet Freedom*, pp. 143–53.

Questions

1. What reasons might some trades unions have for deterring women from pursuing equality claims?
2. Why has economic recession not brought women increased support from the unions?
3. How does the 'history of trade unionism' help to account for the limited participation of women in unions?

☐ What to Do?

The cartoon may give you some ideas about why some trades unions and their meetings are not 'woman friendly'. In spite of this you will note, from the table, that some unions still have a large female membership, although you will also note that their representation at higher levels of union organisation does not reflect the membership pattern.

Reading 8

From Labour Research Department, *Part-time Workers*, p. 13, n/d

Women in the unions. Figures in brackets show how many women there would be if they were represented according to their share of the membership

Union	Membership			Executive members		Full time officials		TUC delegates	
	Total	F	%F	Total	F	Total	F	Total	F
APEX (Professional, Executive, Clerical, Computer)	150,000	77,000	51%	15	1(8)	55	2(28)	15	4(8)
ASTMS (Technical, Managerial)	472,000	82,000	17%	24	2(4)	63	6(11)	30	3(5)
BIFU (Banking, Insurance, Finance)	132,000	64,000	49%	27	3(13)	41	6(20)	20	3(10)
GMWU (General & Municipal)	956,000	327,000	34%	40	0(14)	243	13(83)	73	3(25)
NALGO (Local Govt Officers)	705,000	356,000	50%	70	14(35)	165	11(83)	72	15(36)
NUPE (Public Employees)	700,000	470,000	67%	26	8(17)	150	7(101)	32	10(22)
NUT (Teachers)	258,000	170,000	66%	44	4(29)	43	3(28)	36	7(24)
UNTGW (Tailor & Garment)	117,000	108,000	92%	15	5(14)	47	9(43)	17	7(16)
TGWU (Transport & General)	2,070,000	330,000	16%	39	0(6)	600	9(96)	85	6(14)
USDAW (Shop, Distributive, Allied)	462,000	281,000	63%	16	3(10)	162	13(102)	38	8(24)
TOTALS	6,022,000	2,265,000	38%	316	40(150)	1,569	76(595)	418	66(174)

All figures are approximate and the most recent that were available in November 1980.

A. Coote and B. Campbell, *Sweet Freedom*, p. 167.

Questions

1. List some of the reasons that may inhibit women from attending union meetings.
2. Which unions have a majority of female members?
3. Draw up an 'action plan' for one of these unions to
   (a) increase female participation in ordinary union activities
   (b) increase the number of women in positions of power within the union.
4. How effective do you consider your action plan would be, and why?

Essay Questions

1. With respect to *one* area of public policy discuss the assumptions about women and men that shape policies in this area and assess their impact on women.
2. 'Discrimination is part of the structures and institutions of society.' Discuss in relation to gender inequality in either
   (a) formal politics or
   (b) trades unions.
3. 'Where power is, women are not.' Discuss.

Further Reading

J. Evans, 'Women and Politics: a reappraisal', *Political Studies*, vol. 28, no. 2, 1980. A feminist re-examination of political science research that has led to assumptions about women's public political behaviour.

J. Lovenduski, *Women and European Politics*. Although this covers all European countries, they are separated out in the text so that the reader does not need to consider them all. The amount of information on Britain is too limited to make it very useful in that respect, but it is useful for information on other countries, for comparison of political behaviour, trades unions and public policy.

L. Middleton, *Women in the Labour Movement*. Excellent accounts of women's struggles for decent pay and the franchise during the nineteenth and early twentieth centuries.

P. Norris, *Politics and Sexual Equality*. A comparative account of women's economic, social and political positions in western democracies. It contains much empirical data.

G. Pascall, *Social Policy: A Feminist Analysis*. Besides housing, the areas of social policy discussed in terms of how they affect women include the family, education, health and social security. A lot of detail but easy to read and interesting.

V. Randall, *Women and Politics*. This is a very good book for overall coverage of the material discussed in this chapter – women's political behaviour; women in political elites and policy-making and its impact on women.

J. Siltanen and M. Stanworth (eds), *Women and the Public Sphere*. Some good sociological chapters on women and unions and women and electoral politics. Not all the chapters are easy to read.

M. Stacey and M. Price, *Women, Power and Politics*. A good, clear discussion of the nature of power, women's exclusion from power and the relationship of women to both public and private power bases.

8 | Women together

If women are not particularly visible in formal political institutions they are certainly active in the movements and activities outside these, in protest and ad hoc groups dedicated to bringing about either small-scale or national and international change. The 'Women's Movement' itself has usually avoided all conventional political organisation forms – it has no formal membership, no committees, and no constitution. All women who attempt to eradicate inequality may be said to be part of this movement and as individuals and in groups they have been responsible both for 'putting issues on the agenda' (e.g. rape, domestic violence, abortion) and for keeping issues alive during the decades of this century (e.g. equal pay, married women's property rights).

Many of the activities, though, are poorly documented or little discussed, and this is especially true of the activities of black women who have always been active in communities and have a long tradition of resistance. Bryan *et al.* (1985) describe the money-lending and savings schemes that provided the only available finance for black people when self-help was necessary, and they maintain that the stereotypes of passivity and resistance applied to black women hide the fact that their very survival, from slavery onwards, has depended on militant responses.

Women are popularly seen as the custodians of society's values and hence in need of protection, so when women assert themselves politically as women, and do not at the same time hold fast to their domestic roles, they can receive rough treatment, as the first extract from a Greenham Common protester describes. The concern with peace is a noticeable feature of contemporary feminism and this is important because it is a challenge to the dominant 'masculine' values of war, military spending and aggression; and also because the peace protesters eschew hierarchical organisations and leadership roles, and this places the institutions that attempt to deal with them in a quandary. Greenham is important to many feminists because it has proved capable of drawing so many women into political protest and action.

Although it is the 'male principle' of materialism, waste, alienation, domination and possession that is being challenged, Segal in the second extract warns against seeing the 'masculine' elements of the dominant culture as a 'natural' psychological or emotional attribute of men; this would simply be a variant of the biological determinism that has been disputed, with regard to women, in Chapter 1. Nuclear disarmament may seem only to be related to women in the sense that women are visible in protesting against it, but many feminists have pointed out that the resources consumed by military spending, if diverted to welfare, could transform women's lives both inside and outside the home. Some feminists also connect the ideologies and practices of militarism with those of 'masculinity'. The women's peace movement is therefore important sociologically at the levels both of action and ideology.

Another protest by women that has been obvious, and unprecedented, in recent years has been the Women Against Pit Closures group formed in 1984 in support of the miners' strike. This example of protest also raises the crucial sociological problem of the relationship between class and gender. Stead, in the third extract, maintains that the women's action was a class-based one in support of the men: yet it could also be maintained that the women, in attempting to defend their communities and their children's futures, were in one sense acting as women with particular responsibilities and concerns, and as women they were visible and active in their own right especially as the strike progressed. The media, though, tended to report the women's actions merely as supportive of the men's struggle or, later, as a temporary aberration in a time of crisis.

The fourth extract from an account of a woman involved in the Barnsley Women Against Pit Closures group describes the effects on her own life. Although the women in these groups would not usually describe themselves as 'feminists' it might be interesting for you to consider whether the challenges the groups made and the consciousness that developed could have occurred without the wider influences of feminism and the women's movement. The role of women's domestic labour in connection with male occupations such as mining has been mentioned (see Chapter 2) and this is important in understanding the context and history of this particular case.

The importance of considering gender, theoretically, has been seen as necessary in terms of producing adequate sociological explanations. The question of whether feminists themselves should have a unique and specific approach to sociology is a current debate. Most academic feminists agree that part of their task is to uncover and criticise sexism in their subjects but, in sociology, there is discussion about whether there is a particular methodology that can be construed as feminist and, if so, whether or not it is only the prerogative of female researchers. Much of the knowledge we have of women's cultures and experiences has been gained by qualitative methods, as has our knowledge of men's cultures and experiences, and in the fifth extract Finch discusses the ease with which a female researcher can usually talk to other women – for structural as well as experiential reasons. This raises, as she points out, particular ethical and moral problems that the traditional sociological literature has not touched on.

The importance of knowing about gender divisions and processes has also been described as a requirement in order to produce satisfactory explanations. The way empirical data are collected, which questions are asked, what use is made of the data and so on are all important considerations in extending that knowledge. The last extract by Stanley and Wise puts forward one view of feminist methodology, and although there may be disagreement about this all feminist sociologists see the importance of asserting the validity of women's experience and attempt to incorporate that experience into the definition of the nature and reality.

□ Women
Take
Action

This account of the importance of women's action at Greenham Common was written by a socialist feminist who contrasts women's action there with activities in formal groups. In discussing the Greenham women's support for the Women Against Pit Closures group she mentions the connection between the run-down of the coal industry and the development of nuclear power. Thus, although very different kinds of groups they are both concerned with a national policy and its effects at different levels. The peace protesters are concerned with national and international policies and the women against pit closures with national energy policies affecting their livelihoods and communities. You might also consider constrasting this account with the representations of these women at Greenham as portrayed in the mass media, remembering the points made in Chapter 6.

Reading 1

In many ways Greenham has been a place where a lot of cross-fertilizing has gone on between different groupings of the women's movement. Often trade unionism and life in local councils and political parties drains us of energy. Involvement with the women's peace movement energizes us because of the explosion of women's imagination there, uncramped by men, expressed in a sense of fun and bold, breathtaking actions. Meetings at the camp have led to a widening network of campaigns. During the miners' strike, Greenham women throughout the country spoke at rallies, picketed, raised money for Women Against Pit Closures, and generally supported women in the mining communities in finding their own ways to fight the government and defend the strike. It was women who stressed the connexion between the run-down of the coal industry and massive spending on nuclear power. . . .

Thirty thousand women 'embraced the base' in December 1982. The first Cruise missiles arrived in 1983, each with fifteen times the destructive force of the bomb which destroyed Hiroshima. This was a serious reverse for all the women who were active around Greenham – but the camp survived and the number of support groups grew. Whereas among socialist groups reverses often lead to destructive in-fighting and denunciations, the close-knit Greenham groups have staying power precisely because the women in them deal with their feelings and take care of each other.

Since the 'defensive' effectiveness of Cruise missiles depends on their unseen mobility, the continued existence of the peace camp has limited their activity. . . . The Greenham women, backed up by an organization called 'Cruisewatch', have made each missile journey public, and have slowed its progress. They have kept the existence of Cruise missiles under Reagan's sole control a central political issue in this country. They have drawn attention to the American occupation here, to the 100 and more American bases patrolled by gun-carrying US soldiers. Their protest has placed pressure on the Labour Party, and pushed public opinion to the point where a majority of people now think that the government should tell the American government to remove its Cruise missiles from British soil.

The nine-mile perimeter fence round the USAF base at Greenham is a patchwork of darns, a symbol of army fallibility and peace women's determination. Women have borrowed army jeeps and buses, carried watchtowers outside the fence, covered the base in slogans and decorations, planted trees and flowers. Women have lived undetected inside the base for a week at a time, and with the help of bolt cutters go in and out of the base as they choose.

Those women who 'trespass' repeatedly inside the base or damage the fence are now receiving longer and longer prison sentences: periods of up to a year are becoming common. There are very few women left at the camp, and their health has been strained to the limit. One woman was run over by a missile transporter and had her leg broken; others have been attacked by vigilantes from Newbury and 'unofficial' army patrols, and have suffered cracked ribs and skulls. . . . It is amazing that there are still women living at the camp. They are evicted by bailiffs, sometimes as many as three times a day, and have perfected a system of moving the essentials of life on prams and trolleys, out of reach of the 'muncher' – a refuse-disposal truck that grinds up any bedding, food and so on not carried by a woman. Through rain and cold women live in benders of branches and plastic sheeting which can be easily moved and made again.

For many women throughout the country, the survival of a women's camp against such odds has been an important factor in counteracting despair. . . . The women's camp at Greenham Common has made denial of the existence of nuclear weapons impossible; it has been a constructive channel for anger against this threat to our existence; it has become a symbol of women's ability to take action.

Sue Finch, with Mary, Cynthia, Linda, Colleen, Barbara, Jan, in *Feminist Review No. 23*, pp. 96–9.

Questions

1. What do the authors perceive as the achievements of the women at Greenham Common?
2. Do you think that the women's camp at Greenham Common has 'become a symbol of women's ability to take action'? Give reasons for your answer.
3. Which ideologies and assumptions are the women challenging?

☐ 'Masculinity', 'Femininity' and War

Segal is concerned here to point out that although militarism and masculinity are connected, it is not through the inherent attributes of men but the stereotyped and culturally patterned behaviour. The 'nurturant' aspects of women that some feminists wish to promote are equally a product of women's structural position and to see either men's or women's behaviour as 'natural' is a version of the biological explanations outlined in Chapter 1.

Reading 2

The Greenham filter is right to perceive that military values are 'manly' values. They promote the 'rational' use of force, skill and technology to establish power over others. Military institutions, at least in their most visible form, exist to preserve and train men in the use of violence: to kill, maim and otherwise coerce, discipline and harm other people on orders, as requested, without explanation. They are, it would seem the quintessence of male power. But such a feminist filter fails to perceive much that is also important to any understanding of modern warfare, nuclear missiles and the arms race. Descriptions of the 'needs' and 'mentality' of men leave us with no analysis of modern militarism and its current threat. Wars do not occur because men are eager to fight; on the contrary, military aggression always requires carefully controlled and systematic propaganda, at state level, which plays upon public fears, vulnerabilities, pride and prejudice. . . .

The military has never, and now less than ever, been able to rely upon men's supposed needs and mentality to obtain the number and quality of recruits it would like, without the help of 'economic conscription' through unemployment. The male image of militarism, jealously guarded, also serves to deny or obscure women's relation to nationalism and militarism. . . .

And were a 'killing instinct' a part of man's heritage, we would have to conclude that modern man is remarkably ambivalent about his legacy. Boxing and wrestling may have their fans, and some men may still enjoy the violence and aggression of direct combat, but killing is not popular. . . .

Of all the biological mythologies that surround human behaviour and social arrangements, the one that 'man' is inevitably aggressive, whereas 'woman' is not, is the most tenacious. . . .

There are two aspects of modern warfare that feminists in particular need to analyse: the essential role of ideologies of sexual difference in the preparations and productions for war and the continuing and increasing relation of women to the technologies of war. . . .

The toughening up of the male combat recruit is not only a preparation for military practices, but also necessary to maintain the image of 'military manhood' as the pinnacle of manly daring, the image necessary to attract new recruits eager to prove themselves 'proper men'. The image helps sustain the morale and self-esteem of the men already in uniform, most of whom, much of the time, will lead lives of relentless subservience, obedience and passive dependence – characteristics more typically attributed to 'women'. . . .

Women now compose nearly 10 per cent of the American armed forces, and nearly 5 per cent of the British. Difficulties in recruiting manpower at the educational levels necessary in modern armies and falling birth rates in industrial nations mean that those numbers are likely to rise. There is continuing pressure on military institutions to enlist more women.

The threat this poses to military strategies is not that women fall short as good and useful military recruits, not at all, as we should know from the role of women in guerrilla and liberation armies around the world. It is rather that women's presence in the established armed forces of the state threatens the maintenance of that 'masculine' image of military life essential for the morale and incentive of men. . . .

I do not dismiss the very real hopes of many women and men that it is women who will, in the last resort, do most to save us from the ultimate catastrophe to which militarism and the arms race seem headed: the intentional or unintentional extermination of life on earth. We may be forced to agree that women share in the patriotism and commitment to national interest which sustains militarism and condones war. We may have to agree that neither men's biology nor men's psychology, in themselves, explain the entrenchment of arms production in capitalist and state bureaucratic societies. We may even agree that it is feminist rejection, rather than affirmation, of notions of the separate and different nature and greater vulnerability of women which most threatens the morale of men at arms and the motivation for militaristic thinking. We may agree on all these things, and yet we may still appeal to women's values, to maternal values, to save humanity. However much the supposed peacefulness of women may have failed anti-war feminists in the past, might it not this time be easier for women to see and to challenge the global destruction which so mocks their reproductive and nurturing role?

L. Segal, *Is the Future Female?*, pp. 178–96.

Questions

1. Summarise the main arguments of this passage.
2. 'Were a "killing instinct" part of *man's* heritage, we should have to

conclude that modern man is remarkably ambivalent about his legacy.'
Discuss the evidence both for and against this view.
3. Why might it now be easier for 'women to see and challenge the global
destruction which mocks their reproductive and nurturing roles'?

□ No Intellectuals in the Soup Kitchens

Miners' wives may have little choice about their role, and thus it
was in their interests to defend the miners' jobs. Stead maintains
that the women who fought against pit closures were fighting a
'class' rather than a 'gender' battle, but you might want to consider
the extent to which you agree with this. It was, though, a working-
class women's protest and for this reason is important.

Reading 3

In 1987, when the pits as well as the people who work in them are
being scrapped in favour of nuclear power, the women are also
becoming less necessary to the industry, although they have always
shown a loyalty to their husbands' work, to the local mines and to the
very seams of coal within them.

The miners' wives are in a unique quandary. They are a necessary
part of a skilled manual job in which they can never participate and in
most cases do not even want to. Outside mining, women can be
teachers, executives and even Church ministers. They have a
choice. The miner's wife has no choice. That is why, during the strike,
mining women in the support groups were so insistent that the strike
was producing a totally new women's movement, that it was the first
to have its roots in the working class. . . .

In their bones they had always known they were exploited but they
knew that at least their exploitation paralleled that of the men they
shared their lives with. That is why miners' wives don't, on the whole,
take their resentment of the past out on the miners of the present.
They complain about their husbands' prejudices but they are setting
out to change them – in between looking after the kids and getting
the meals ready for the end of the shift. . . .

The women in 1984–85 were determined that it was going to be a
truly working-class women's movement, and that no one from outside was going to patronise them, which they felt had happened with
upper-class women in 1926.

Florence Anderson of the Eppleton Area Miners' Wives' Support Group in Durham, said after the strike:

> All the women in our support group had connections with the mining community. That was a rule we made at the start. We really didn't want any outsiders in our kitchen, or professional do-gooders. We said it wasn't going to be like 1926, with people shuffling up to the soup kitchens demoralised and degraded. It was going to be miners' wives, miners' mothers, miners' sisters serving miners and their wives and families.
>
> We didn't want any sort of intellectuals coming down to play around in soup kitchens. It was a working-class women's movement and that's why we were so proud of it. We kept it like that, because we said coming into the kitchen should be like coming home. Our kitchen was popular because we said everybody had to be made welcome. It was our own feeding our own. There was no feeling about it. We had no outsiders. In fact, we got no help from the Labour Party in Hetton at all. All we had from the Hetton Labour Party, in a mining community, was half the proceeds of a dance held in November, and we contributed to that because we all went along there and sat at the back and were never even mentioned. I think the Labour Party wasn't more involved because the miners' wives got together and took the lead from the start.

J. Stead, *Never the Same Again: Women and the Miners' Strike 1984–85*, pp. 27–9.

Questions

1. What was different about the 1984–5 pits' dispute that caused the miners to organise nationally?
2. 'In their bones they had always known they were exploited but they knew that at least their exploitation paralleled that of the men they shared their lives with.' Critically discuss this view.
3. Why did the miners' wives support group not want 'outsiders' in their kitchens?

□ 'It Changed my Life.'

This miner's wife from Barnsley describes the effect that the action has had on her and her family. You might like to remind yourself of the fact that in Chapter 2 there was an indication that men do not easily 'role swop' even when made redundant and you might consider whether the circumstances in this case make it a different proposition. This is also an interesting passage because it is one example of ordinary women 'writing their own history'.

Reading 4

It is very difficult to write in a few pages my role as a woman involved in the strike of 84/86. I found at my own union conference in April '84 that my time seemed to be fully occupied rounding up financial and moral support for the miners amongst the delegates there, with two miners from Kent. . . . On my return I went on the marvellous women's rally in Barnsley and joined the Women Against Pit Closures Group. This not only completely changed my life and my role, but also that of my family. As I worked part time in the evenings they were quite used to me being at home during the day, cooking, cleaning and shopping. They had to adjust overnight to my never being at home, virtually popping in and out and their home being turned into a storage centre for food, clothes and mountains of leaflets and literature. My mother, who is seventy eight, took over the washing and ironing and many times despaired that the house was so full of boxes of all sorts of things we didn't even have enough room to vacuum. The laugh used to be, 'look, leave the cobwebs, they'll look great at Christmas sprayed with silver and gold.'

With other women of our community we opened a soup kitchen. This work was 'enhanced' by going picketing all over the coalfield, attending rallies and meetings and going into the larger cities of the country, speaking at meetings not only to raise further monies, but to express our heartfelt thanks for the support they had already given.

At the end of August we had our first scab at Woolley Colliery. Again I found that there was something to be done to fill my empty hours! Not only did I start to picket locally, but we started to provide soup for the pickets. My day now started at five a.m. and I was lucky if I finished at twelve thirty a.m. Hello the nineteen or twenty hour day! The policing at Woolley Colliery suddenly intensified. Riot police, dogs and horses invaded our estates and communities which were miles away from the colliery entrance. Someone gave us a small caravan to make our soup distribution easier and warmer (prior to this we had served it outside on a wall). What a threat we women must have been to the riot police – serving soup to the pickets. They found it such a threat they found it necessary to surround our little caravan with police dogs. Their noses on our serving counter, growling and snapping virtually imprisoning us, but they found they could neither frighten or deter us, we carried on making soup and still appeared the next day. . . .

I am not a writer and am only able to touch briefly on my experiences during the strike, but I do know that it certainly enhanced my life, broadened my outlook in regard to politics, trade unions and education. I am humbled and proud to know that I was involved in this great piece of history. . . .

Even though the strike is over, many women are still working as hard and as many hours a day as before to further our cause. The most misguided statement I have made was that when the strike was over I would be able to catch up on my housework and decorating. That day is yet to come. I don't think I'll ever be able to do all I have got to in the next few months! But I have a purpose in life, many aims and goals to achieve now which I never had before, and so, dear reader, as time presses and the days fly by, my next commitment demands that I now put away pen and paper without delay.

Barnsley Miners' Wives Action Group, *We Struggled to Laugh*, pp. 10–12.

Questions

1. Would you expect the experiences of these women to have resulted in more long-term changes in their perceptions and behaviour? Give reasons for your answer.
2. To what extent do you consider that the actions of the miners' wives were either an extension of their domestic role or an extension of their role as women?

☐ The Interviewer as a Friendly Guest

In order to find out more about both women themselves and gender structures we must collect empirical data. There are many ways of doing this but none raises as many problems for researchers as qualitative methods, including interviewing. This particular method also raises ethical and moral problems for feminist researchers researching women, as this extract illustrates. An earlier excerpt by the same author (see Chapter 2) was from a book in which she discusses some of her research on clergy wives and her discussion here about the collection of the data illustrates the research processes that occur before a 'final version' appears.

Reading 5

My experience of interviewing has raised a combination of method-ological, personal, political and moral issues, upon which I find it necessary to reflect both as a sociologist and as a feminist. These issues have become focused by considering the extreme ease with which, in my experience, a woman researcher can elicit material from other women. That in turn raises ethical and political questions which I have found some difficulty in resolving. One reason for this difficulty is that discussions of the 'ethics' of research are commonly conducted within a framework which is drawn from the public do-main of men, and which I find at best unhelpful in relation to research with women. . . .

Both the clergymen's wives and the playgroups studies were concerned entirely with women; in both I used qualitative techniques including in-depth interviewing; and in both I talked to women in their own homes about aspects of their lives which centrally defined their identities as women – marriage, motherhood and childrearing. . . .

I claim no special personal qualities which make it peculiarly easy for me to get people to talk, but women whom I have interviewed often are surprised at the ease with which they do talk in the interview situation. One woman in my playgroup study (who told me that she was so chronically shy that when she had recently started a new job it had taken her a week to pluck up courage to ask how to find the toilet), said after her interview that she had surprised herself – it had not really felt, she said, as if she was talking to a stranger. . . . a feeling which was very common among the women I interviewed in both studies [was] that they had found this interview a welcome experience in contrast with the lack of opportunities to talk about themselves in this way in other circumstances. Some variation on the comment 'I've really enjoyed having someone to talk to' was made at the end of many interviews.

How far does this experience simply reflect the effectiveness of in-depth interviewing styles *per se*, and how far is it specific to women? It seems to me that there are grounds for expecting that where a woman researcher is interviewing other women, this is a situation with special characteristics conducive to the easy flow of information. Firstly, women mostly are more used than men to ac-cepting intrusions through questioning into the more private parts of their lives, including during encounters in their own homes. Through their experience of motherhood they are subject to questioning from doctors, midwives and health visitors; and also from people such as housing visitors, insurance agents and social workers, who deal principally with women as the people with imputed responsibility for home and household. As subjects of research, therefore, women are less likely than men to find questions about their lives unusual and therefore inadmissible. Secondly, in the setting of the interviewee's own home, an interview conducted in an informal way by another woman can easily take on the character of an intimate conversation. The interviewee feels quite comfortable with this precisely because the interviewer is acting as a friendly guest, not an official inquisitor; and the model is, in effect, an easy, intimate relationship between two women.

Thirdly, the structural position of women, and in particular their consignment to the privatised, domestic sphere makes it particularly likely that they will welcome the opportunity to talk to a sympathetic listener. The experience of loneliness was common to women in both my studies. . . .

The moral dilemmas which I have experienced in relation to the use of the data thus created have emerged precisely because the situation of a woman interviewing women *is* special, and is easy only because my identity as a woman makes it so. I have, in other words, traded on that identity. I have also emerged from interviews with the feeling that my interviewees need to know how to protect themselves from people like me. They have often revealed very private parts of their lives in return for what must be, in the last resort, very flimsy guarantees of confidentiality. . . .

There is therefore a real exploitative potential in the easily established trust between women, which makes women especially vulnerable as subjects of research. The effectiveness of in-depth interviewing techniques when used by women researchers to study other women is undoubtedly a great asset in creating sociological knowledge which encompasses and expresses the experiences of women. But the very effectiveness of these techniques leaves women open to exploitation of various kinds through the research process. That exploitation is not simply that these techniques can be used by other than *bona fide* researchers: but it is an ever-present possibility for the most serious and morally upright of researchers, feminists included. It seems to me that the crux of this exploitative potential lies in the relationship established between interviewer and interviewee.

J. Finch, in C. Bell and H. Roberts (eds), *Social Researching*, pp. 71–81.

Questions

1. Why is a woman researcher interviewing women 'conducive to the flow of information'?
2. What are the moral and ethical dilemmas that the author describes in relation to women researching women?
3. Many 'methods' textbooks emphasise 'objectivity' and warn against 'over-rapport' with the respondents: critically discuss this as a methodological issue in relation to interviewing.

☐ A Sociology for Women rather than of Women

Research on women is necessary to 'fill the gaps' in our knowledge but if the theories and conclusions (discussed in Chapter 1) remain unchanged and women are simply added-in to pre-existing ideas we still have a masculine sociology. So should feminist research be *by* women and *for* women? This is one particular view and you might consider whether women can always do research on men – which these authors claim is necessary – and what control researchers have over their findings to ensure that they are not used against, rather than for, women. These issues are very much a live debate within sociology.

Reading 6

One implication of feminist criticisms of sexism within the social sciences is that future research ought to be *on* and *for* women, and should be carried out *by* women. Such research is, at least in part, 'corrective'. By this we mean it is largely descriptive and concerned with filling-in gaps in our knowledge about women. . . .

But there are dangers in such an approach. Studying women separately may lead to a 'ghetto effect', because if 'women' are separated-off in this way then feminist work may be seen as having no implication for the rest of the social sciences. We feel that an equal danger is that if such a separation occurs then the social sciences won't influence feminism. . . .

We also have difficulty with the idea that feminist research must be research on women only. If 'sexism' is the name of the problem addressed by feminism then men are importantly involved, to say the least, in its practice. And so we argue that, essential though research specifically on women is, feminist research must not become *confined* to this. Feminist research must be concerned with all aspects of social reality and all participants in it. It seems obvious to us that any analysis of women's oppression *must* involve research on the part played by men in this.

Although we find problems with research exclusively 'on women', we see an emphasis on research *by* women as absolutely fundamental to feminist research. We reject the idea that men can be feminists because we argue that what is essential to 'being feminist' is the possession of 'feminist consciousness'. And we see feminist consciousness as rooted in the concrete, practical and everyday experiences of being, and being treated as, *a woman*. Feminist consciousness is a particular kind of interpretation of the experience of being a woman as this is presently constructed in sexist society. No men know what it is to be treated as a woman; and even fewer interpret such treatment in the ways we define as central to 'feminist consciousness'.

Closely associated with the interpretation of feminist research as research on women and by women is the notion that it ought also to be research *for* women. The product of feminist research should be directly used by women in order to formulate policies and provisions necessary for feminist activities.

L. Stanley and S. Wise, *Breaking Out: Feminist Consciousness and Feminist Research*, pp. 17–19.

Questions

1. Why do the authors consider that feminist researchers should also study men?
2. What might be the methodological difficulties and/or advantages of a woman researcher studying men?
3. Do you agree with the assertion that men cannot be feminists because they have never been treated as women?
4. To what extent is it possible for feminist research to be used by other women to 'formulate policies necessary for feminist activities'?

Essay Questions

1. Assess the importance of *either* the Women's Peace Movement *or* the Women Against Pit Closures group as vehicles for women's political action.
2. Is it possible to have a 'feminist methodology'?

3. 'Female experience affirms that class oppression and gender oppression are related in many ways, but they are not the same.' Discuss.

Further Reading

M. Ali, 'The Coal War: women's struggle during the miners' strike', in R. Ridd and H. Callaway (eds), *Caught up in Conflict*. A clear account of the background to the dispute and the development of the women's organisation as the strike progressed.

B. Bryan, S. Dadzie and S. Scafe, *Heart of the Race: Black Women's Lives in Britain*. This book discusses the contribution of black women to areas of policy that affect them. Although not a sociological account the historical background of the struggles of black women is important.

J. Finch, 'It's great to have someone to talk to', in C. Bell and H. Roberts (eds), *Social Researching: Politics, Problems and Practice*. It is worth reading the whole chapter from which the extract has been taken as it is interesting and pertinent.

H. Graham, 'Do her answers fit his questions? Women and the survey method' in E. Gamarnikow *et al.* (eds), *The Public and the Private*. A consideration of survey, as opposed to qualitative, methods within a feminist framework.

L. Jones, *Keeping the Peace*. Interesting personal accounts of women organising for peace in different ways.

S. Leyland, 'Greenham women are everywhere' in J. Holland (ed.) *Feminist Action 1*. A personal account of the author's involvement in organising the large encircling of Greenham base in 1982.

L. Loach, 'We'll be here right to the end – and after: women in the miners' strike', in H. Beynon (ed.), *Digging Deeper*. A short account of women in the pits' dispute which mentions some of the issues and has examples of the effect on particular women.

M. Mayo, *Women in the Community*. Case studies of community action, of a less publicised kind, by women.

L. McKee and M. O'Brien, 'Interviewing men', in E. Garmarnikow *et al.* (eds), *The Public and the Private*. An account from their own research on fathers of how gender influences the research process and the implications of this for what information is pursued or neglected.

Bibliography

Acker, S. 'Sociology, gender and education', in S. Acker *et al.*, *Women and Education*, Kogan Page, 1984.

Ali, M. 'The coal war: women's struggle during the miners' strike', in R. Ridd and H. Callaway (eds), *Caught up in Conflict*, Macmillan, 1986.

Allen, G. *Family Life*, Basil Blackwell, 1985.

Amos, V. and Parmar, P. 'Resistances and responses: the experience of black girls in Britain', in A. McRobbie and T. McCabe (eds), *Feminism for Girls*, Routledge & Kegan Paul, 1981.

Anyon, J. 'Intersections of gender and class', in S. Walker and L. Barton, *Gender, Class and Education*, Falmer Press, 1983.

Ardener, S., *Defining Females*, Croom Helm, 1978.

Banks, O. *Faces of Feminism*, Martin Robertson, 1981.

Barker, D. and Allen, S. (eds), *Dependence and Exploitation in Work and Marriage*, Longman, 1976.

Barnsley Miners' Wives Action Group, *We Struggled to Laugh*, 1987.

Barrett, M. and McIntosh, M. *The Anti-Social Family*, Verso, 1982.

Bell, C. 'Work, non-work and unemployment – a discussion', in R. Burgess (ed.), *Exploring Society*, Longman, 1986.

Belotti, E. *Little Girls*, Writers and Readers Cooperative, 1975.

Berger, J. *Ways of Seeing*, Penguin, 1972.

Bhavnani, K.K. and Coulson, M. 'Transforming socialist feminism: the challenge of racism', *Feminist Review* no. 23, June 1986.

Bowles, S. and Gintis, H. *Schooling in Capitalist America*, Routledge & Kegan Paul, 1976.

Broadbent, L. *et al.* (Glasgow Media Group), *War and Peace News*, Open University Press, 1985.

Bryan, B., Dadzie, S. and Scafe, S. *The Heart of the Race: Black Women's Lives in Britain*, Virago, 1985.

Burgoyne, J. and Clark, D. *Making a Go of It: A Study of Step-Families in Sheffield*, Routledge & Kegan Paul, 1984.

Buswell, C. 'Training for low pay', in C. Glendinning and J. Millar (eds), *Women and Poverty*, Wheatsheaf, 1987.

Campbell, A. *Girl Delinquents*, Basil Blackwell, 1981.

Campbell, B. *Wigan Pier Revisited*, Virago, 1984.

Chetwynd, J. and Hartnett, O. *The Sex Role System*, Routledge & Kegan Paul, 1978.

Close, P. and Collins, R. *Family and Economy in Modern Britain*, Macmillan, 1985.

Connell, R.W. 'Theorising gender', *Sociology*, vol. 19, no. 2, May 1985.

Coote, A. and Campbell, B. *Sweet Freedom*, Basil Blackwell, 1982.

De Beauvoir, S. *The Second Sex*, Cape, 1953.

Deem, R. *Schooling for Women's Work*, Routledge & Kegan Paul, 1980.

Deem, R. *Coeducation Reconsidered*, Open University Press, 1984.

Delamont, S. *The Sociology of Women*, Allen & Unwin, 1980.
Delamont, S. *Sex Roles and the School*, Methuen, 1980.
Dex, S. *Women's Work Histories: An Analysis of the Women and Employment Survey*, Research paper no. 46, Department of Employment, 1984.
Drake, B. *Women in Trade Unions*, Virago, 1984.
Epstein, T.S. *et al., Women, Work and Family in Britain and Germany*, Croom Helm, 1986.
Evans, J. 'Women and politics: a reappraisal', *Political Studies*, vol. 28, no. 2, 1980.
Evans, M. (ed.), *The Woman Question*, Fontana, 1982.
Ferguson, M. *Forever Feminine: Women's Magazines and the Cult of Femininity*, Heinemann, 1983.
Finch, J. *Married to the Job*, Allen & Unwin, 1983.
Finch, J. 'It's great to have someone to talk to: the ethics and politics of interviewing women', in C. Bell and H. Roberts (eds), *Social Researching*, Routledge & Kegan Paul, 1984.
Finch, S. with Mary, Cynthia, Linda, Colleen, Barbara, Jan, 'Socialist-feminists and Greenham', *Feminist Review*, no. 23, June 1986.
Firestone, S., *The Dialectic of Sex*, The Women's Press, 1979.
Fransella, F. and Frost, K. *On Being a Woman*, Tavistock, 1977.
Frith, G. 'Little women, good wives: is English good for girls?' in A. McRobbie and T. McCabe (eds), *Feminism for Girls*, Routledge & Kegan Paul, 1981.
Fuller, M. 'Black girls in a London comprehensive school', in R. Deem (ed.), *Schooling for Womens's Work*, Routledge & Kegan Paul, 1980.
Game, A. and Pringle, R. *Gender at Work*, Pluto Press, 1984.
Garnsey, E., Rubery, J. and Wilkinson, F. 'Labour market structure and work-force divisions', in R. Deem and G. Salaman (eds), *Work, Culture and Society*, Open University Press, 1985.
Gittens, D. *Fair Sex: Family Size and Social Structure 1900–39*, Hutchinson, 1982.
Gittens, D. *The Family in Question*, Macmillan, 1985.
Godwin, A. 'Early years in the Trade Unions', in L. Middleton (ed.), *Women in the Labour Movement*, Croom Helm, 1977.
Graham, H. 'Do her answers fit his questions? Women and the survey method', in E. Gamarnikow *et al.* (eds), *The Public and the Private*, Heinemann, 1983.
Griffin, C. *Typical Girls?*, Routledge & Kegan Paul, 1985.
Hall, S. and Jefferson, T. *Resistance through Rituals*, Hutchinson, 1976.
Harding, J. 'Sex differences in performance in science examinations', in R. Deem, *Schooling for Women's Work*, Routledge & Kegan Paul, 1980.
Herzog, M. *From Hand to Mouth: Women and Piecework*, Penguin, 1980.
Hobson, D. 'Housewives and the mass media', in S. Hall *et al.*, *Culture, Media, Language*, Hutchinson, 1980.
Jenkins, R. *Lads, Citizens and Ordinary Kids*, Routledge & Kegan Paul, 1983.
Jones, L. *Keeping the Peace*, The Women's Press, 1983.
King, J. and Stott, M. *Is this Your Life? Images of Women in the Media*, Virago, 1977.

Kuhn, J. 'Working at the superstore', in T.S. Epstein, K. Crehan, A. Genzer and J. Sass (eds), *Women, Work and Family in Britain and Germany*, Croom Helm, 1986.

Lees, S. *Losing Out: Sexuality and Adolescent Girls*, Hutchinson, 1986.

Leonard, D. *Sex and Generation: A Study of Courtship and Weddings*, Tavistock, 1980.

Leonard, D. and Hood Williams, J. *Families*, Macmillan, 1988.

Leyland, S. 'Greenham women are everywhere', in J. Holland (ed.), *Feminist Action I*, Battleaxe Books, 1984.

Loach, L. 'We'll be here right to the end – and after: women in the miners' strike', in H. Beynon (ed.), *Digging Deeper*, Verso, 1985.

Lovenduski, J. *Women and European Politics*, Wheatsheaf, 1986.

Malos, E. (ed.), *The Politics of Housework*, Allison & Busby, 1980.

Maymay, P. and Simpson, R. 'Three female roles in television commercials', *Sex Roles*, vol. 7, no. 12, 1981.

Mayo, M. *Women in the Community*, Routledge & Kegan Paul, 1977.

McKee, L and O'Brien, M. 'Interviewing men', in E. Gamarnikow *et al.* (eds), *The Public and the Private*, Heinemann, 1983.

McQuail, D. *Mass Communication Theory: An Introduction*, Sage, 1983.

McRobbie, A. 'Jackie: An ideology of adolescent femininity', in B. Waites, T. Bennett and G. Martin (eds), *Popular Culture Past and Present*, Croom Helm, 1982.

McRobbie, A. and McCabe, T. *Feminism for Girls*, Routledge & Kegan Paul, 1981.

Meyenn, R. 'School girls' peer groups', in P. Woods (ed.), *Pupil Strategies*, Croom Helm, 1980.

Middleton, L. *Women in the Labour Movement*, Croom Helm, 1977.

MORI Poll reported in *New Statesman*, 27 March 1981.

Morley, D. *Family Television: Cultural Power and Domestic Leisure*, Comedia, 1986.

New, C. and David, M. *For the Children's Sake*, Penguin, 1985.

Norris, P. *Politics and Sexual Equality*, Wheatsheaf, 1987.

Oakley, A. *Housewife*, Penguin, 1974.

Oakley, A. *Subject Women*, Martin Robertson, 1981.

Pahl, R.E. *Divisions of Labour*, Basil Blackwell, 1984.

Pascall, G. *Social Policy: A Feminist Analysis*, Tavistock, 1986.

Perkins, T.E. 'Rethinking stereotypes', in M. Barrett *et al.*, *Ideology and Cultural Production*, Croom Helm, 1979.

Pollert, A. *Girls, Wives, Factory Lives*, Macmillan, 1981.

Randall, V. *Women and Politics*, Macmillan, 1982.

Roberts, B. *et al.*, *New Approaches to Economic Life*, Manchester University Press, 1985.

Roberts, H. *Doing Feminist Research*, Routledge & Kegan Paul, 1981.

Robinson, O. 'The changing labour market: the phenomenon of part-time work in Britain', *National Westminster Bank Quarterly Review*, November 1985.

Sanders, D. and Reed, J. *Kitchen Sink or Swim*, Penguin, 1982.

Sarsby, J. *Romantic Love and Society*, Penguin, 1983.

Segal, L. *Is the Future Female?*, Virago, 1987.

Sharpe, S. *Just Like a Girl: How Girls Learn to be Women*, Penguin, 1976.

Sharpe, S. *Double Identity: The Lives of Working Mothers*, Penguin, 1984.

Sharpe, S. *Falling for Love: Teenage Mothers Talk*, Virago, 1987.

Siltanen, J. and Stanworth, M. *Women and the Public Sphere*, Hutchinson, 1984.

Souhami, D. *A Woman's Place: The Changing Picture of Women in Britain*, Penguin, 1986.

Spender, D. *Invisible Women: The Schooling Scandal*, Writers and Readers Cooperative, 1982.

Stacey, M. and Price, M. *Women, Power and Politics*, Tavistock, 1981.

Stanley, L. and Wise, S. *Breaking Out: Feminist Consciousness and Feminist Research*, Routledge & Kegan Paul, 1983.

Stanworth, M. *Gender and Schooling*, Hutchinson, 1983.

Stead, J. *Never the Same Again: Women and the Miners' Strike 1985*, The Women's Press, 1987.

Walby, S. *Patriarchy at Work*, Polity Press, 1986.

Werneke, D. 'Women: the vulnerable group', in T. Forrester (ed.), *The Information Technology Revolution*, Basil Blackwell, 1985.

West, J. (ed.), *Work, Women and the Labour Market*, Routledge & Kegan Paul, 1982.

Whitelegg, E. *et al.* (eds), *The Changing Experience of Women*, Basil Blackwell, 1986.

Whyte, J. 'Girl friendly science and the girl friendly school', in J. Whyte *et al.*, *Girl Friendly Schooling*, Methuen, 1985.

Williamson, J. *Decoding Advertisements: Ideology and Meaning in Advertising*, Marion Boyars, 1978.

Willis, P. *Learning to Labour*, Saxon House, 1977.

Winship, J. 'A woman's world: *Woman* – an ideal of femininity', in Women's Studies Group, CCCS, *Women Take Issue*, Hutchinson, 1978.

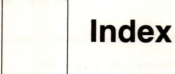

Index

advertisements 97–8
Amos V. & Parmar P. 47–8
Anyon J. 55
Archer J. 7–8

Banks O. 13–14
Barnsley Miners' Wives Action
    Group 135–6
Barrett M. & McIntosh M. 35–6
Belotti E.G. 41–2
Berger J. 93
Bhavnani K. & Coulson
    M. 36–7
biological differences 5, 7–8
Bowles S. & Gintis H. 53
Brown R.K. 16–17
Bryan B., Dadzie S. & Scafe S.
    126
Buswell C. 68–9

Campbell A. 48–50
Campbell B. 50–51
childcare 31–5
childhood, ideology of 21, 23–4
class 6, 7, 24, 55, 133–4, (see
    also 'stratification')
Collins R. 25–6
Connel R.W. 1, 5–6
Coote A. & Campbell B. 121–3

de Beauvoir S. 6
Delamont S. 62–3
Dex S. 76
division of labour 26–30
domestic labour 22, 25–6, (see
    also 'housework')
domesticity, ideology of 21–3,
    24–5, 68–9
Drake B. 117–9

education 53–69
employment 16–17, 30–1, 71–88,

(see also 'labour market' and
    'labour process')
Equal Pay Act 75, 108

family 21–3, 35–7
'family wage' 21
femininity 48–50, 62–3, 98–100,
    130–2
feminist theories 6, 12–14, 35,
    53, 120
Ferguson M. 99–100
Finch J. 30–1, 137–8
Finch S. et. al. 129–30
Firestone S. 14, 15
Fransella F. & Frost K. 11–12
Fuller M. 66–7

Garnsey E, Rubery J. &
    Wilkinson F. 78–80
gender 5–7
gender relations 1, 64–5, 102–5
girls 39–51
Gittins D. 23–5
Godwin A. 119–20

Harding J. 57–8
Hobson D. 100–2
'housewife' 23–5, 100–2
housework 29, (see also
    'domestic labour' and division
    of labour')

income 77, 119–20

knowledge 60–1
Kuhn J. 83–4

labour market 68–9, 78–80,
    84–6, (see also 'employment')
labour process 80–2, 83–4
Lees S. 45–6
love 6, 15, 45

Mamay P. & Simpson R.   97–8
marriage   22, 30–1, 35–6, 46–8
masculinity   39, 130–2
McQuail D.   93
Mc Robbie A.   43–4
media   91–105
militarism   130–2
Morgan D.   18–19
Morley D.   102–5
Morris L.   27–8
motherhood   9–10, 22–3, 50–1

New C. & David M.   33–4
Norris P.   113–5

Oakley A.   9–10

Pahl R.E.   73–5
Pascall G.   115–7
patriarchy   13–14, 53
Perkins T.   94–5
political elites   112–5
political participation   109–12
politics   107–115
protest   126–30
psychological theories   9–10, 24

race   23, 36–7, 46–8, 66–7, 126
Randall V.   110–12
research methods   18–19, 59–60,
   127–8, 136–8, 139–40
reserve army of labour   72
Robinson O.   85–6
romance   43–4

Sanders D. & Reed J.   32–3

Segal L.   131–2
science   57–60
sex   5–7, 14
Sex Discrimination Act   108
sex roles   7, 41–2, 97–8
sexuality   5, 37, 45–6, 64
Sharpe S.   87–8
Siltanen J. & Stanworth M.   110
social policy   21, 24, 33–4, 35,
   50–1, 73–4, 115–17
sociological theory   1, 2, 6–7,
   139–40
Spender D.   60–1
Stanley L. & Wise S.   139–40
Stanworth M.   64–5
State, the   21, 24, 34
Stead J.   133–4
stereotypes   41–2, 47, 55, 93–5
stratification   2, 7, (see also
   'class')
subcultures   48–50, 66–7

technology   22, 59–60, 81–2
trades unions   117–23
training   68–9

unemployment   72

wages   (see 'income')
Walby S.   72
Werneke D.   80–2
Whyte J.   59–60
Williamson J.   92
Willis P.   39
women's movement   126, 133